8 Miles to the Pub

Rambling on from Derby to Malton

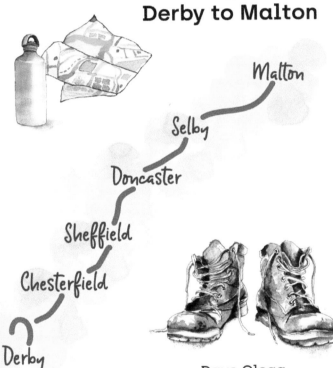

Malton

Selby

Doncaster

Sheffield

Chesterfield

Derby

Dave Clegg
Steve Mullins
David Philpott

8 Miles to the Pub

A walk from Derby to Malton

In easy stages, with attractions

Published by New Generation Publishing in 2020.

First Edition.

ISBN

     Paperback   978-1-80031-723-9
     Ebook   978-1-80031-722-2

www.newgeneration-publishing.com

 New Generation Publishing

Introduction.

This is a story about three 15-year-olds catching up after some 50 years apart having done very different things. Hopefully although we've deteriorated physically, we've kept the curiosity, broad interest and level of (ir)responsibility of an adolescent.

We grew up together in the village of Birkenshaw in the West Riding of Yorkshire, were members of the 1st Spen Valley Scout Group, attended Heckmondwike Grammar School and then went our own ways to different universities and different disciplines.

Dave studied electronics, gained a doctorate and would be good at pub quizzes given twenty minutes between questions. A fount of useless knowledge.

Steve studied biology and then ecological heavy metal and hasn't got a clue what plants are called. Generally found dreaming a few yards behind.

David studied civil engineering, is a chartered engineer, good with bridges and lost some of his map reading cognitive ability. Good at explaining why things are built in a particular way.

This walk was dreamed up after Steve had moved back North and together, we went for a couple of local walks to catch up. As boy scouts some 50-odd years ago, walking, camping and yomping had been regular weekend activities and occasional weeks away for the three of us.

During the couple of walks to catch up we discovered that, despite very different careers, we each had a similar outlook on life and a series of walks seemed like a good way to stay in touch and get some exercise and fresh air from time to time; once a month seemed about right.

As silly old men we thought we still have the youth, resilience and experience to cope. However, no longer is the 40-mile yomp the order of the day and distance is now much less important, provided we cover some ground and, as joints and muscles stiffen, reminiscence, humour and relaxed time together have become more important – and actually achievable. The objective is now a sharing of some of the more formative bits of our growing up, wondering 'what if …' and a bit of whimsey.

We couldn't decide whether this book was going to be a travelogue, a guide book, tourist information or an advert for Yorkshire and North Derbyshire, but it doesn't really matter. For us it is a reflection on the importance of friendship and of the bonds that survive for a lifetime. It is a record of how we three have rekindled a closeness that we had as teenagers, over 50 years ago. We hope that it might inspire you to do the same in whatever form you choose.

Thanks.

Our thanks go to Arthur Wainwright whose Coast to Coast Walk is dedicated to the second person to complete it. He had made it up as he went along; so, if he can, we can.

Happily, we live at three handy points for a long walk: David in Derby, Dave in Sheffield and Steve near Malton which leads to three sections for the journey:

- From Derby to Chesterfield,
- From Chesterfield to Selby, and
- From Selby to Malton.

Each journey is about the same length and which can be divided into several stretches, each of about eight miles, and with a pub at the end of nearly every stretch. Hence the title of the story.

The person whose stretch it was this month would plan and arrange the route as well as the food & drink so that the other two of us just turned up and enjoyed a day's holiday.

That said, some of the planning was a bit seat-of-the-pants and we enjoyed various detours and missed turnings but, after decades of trying to drive the world, we let the world drive us to some extent.

A point to note is that there are no maps included in the story; in the spirit of Wainwright we leave it to those following us to also make it up as they go along. Key landmarks and towns are noted and our reference is the Ordnance Survey *Explorer* series, scaled at 1:25,000 which shows lots of detail and well-defined paths.

Maps and map references are detailed in the section marked 'Personal Log' at the end.

Wherever possible the walks were reached by public transport (avoids drinking and driving), but on occasion two cars were necessary; thankfully these walks are few and far between.

An additional consideration was to take in some culture wherever possible (other than beer) so side journeys to museums, abbeys, and yes, the odd beer festival are described without any apologies.

Due to family or work commitments there were occasions when one of us was unavailable but, as the day had been scheduled the other two of us would enjoy the planned walk.

If you follow our footsteps, we are confident you will have a very fulfilling journey. Enjoy.

3

Contents

Things We Learned or Found of Interest.

That we are not as fit as we used to be.

Daffodils make rubbish way-markers.

There are something like 24 different ways to lay a dry-stone wall.

It's quite steep around Matlock.

Timing is everything.

Rain can bring about a change of route.

The traditional English meadow is alive and well.

Barrow Hill Beer Festival is worth a visit.

Sheffield (England's 5th largest city) is the most wooded in Europe.

Bridge Art is quite creative and often well done.

Viaducts have a thicker upright for safety reasons.

What POOPER stands for.

Primitive Methodists (the Prims) exist.

The devastation caused by flooding.

The width of a standard British cow (about 1.5 metres).

The Stars & Stripes originated in Selby.

Why the Stars & Stripes originated in Selby.

That old railway lines make for easy walking.

How to calculate the weight of rain.

England's tallest man was 7' 9" (2.36 metres).

Pigeons can look bewildered.

We learn what a glebe is.

To respect cows but show who's boss.

Landscape art is big.

Sir Tatton Sykes did some amazing things with Churches.

Wharram Quarry is one of the best nature reserves in Yorkshire.

Decide which side of the river you want to end up on.

You are almost certain to take a wrong turn.

Not all gates have a purpose.

Pubs are not always open when you would like them to be.

Finally, beauty is in the eye of the beholder.

Section 1: Derby to Chesterfield.

It is my pleasure to follow the introduction and detail my post teenage years. I did not have quite the wanderlust of Dave and Steve and studied Civil Engineering at Bradford, graduating in 1970. I still stayed "at home" moving to Bishopthorpe, near York, still in the West Riding until 1st April 1974 when I was re-organised into North Yorkshire.

My career has been wholly in Railways, initially with BR. We were not like the famous curled-up sandwich and did our Engineering very well at minimal cost. Whilst living in York I travelled all over the Eastern side of the Country from King's Cross to the Scottish Border.

I have had a very exciting and fulfilling career, enjoying every day. I am so grateful for this. I have worked on prestigious Civil Engineering Projects, Renewals, Maintenance and Design. I subsequently moved onto interdisciplinary responsibilities involving integration of my own discipline with Signalling, Telecommunications, Electrification and Plant.

In 1991 I moved to Derby for a work opportunity after managing 21 years changing roles and work locations but without moving home! This is now my home and likely to remain so.

The world changed in 1994-6 when BR Privatised and I have helped direct a number of major contractors to develop their Railway skills since. I became a self-employed consultant and am now a lecturer in this topic, putting something back to my discipline.

I had intermittent contact with Dave and Steve over the years (mainly Christmas Card) and in late 2000s arrange to meet Steve in London for a beer after I had had a meeting. And again… When Steve moved back to Yorkshire, the catalyst for the walks occurred. They have been most enjoyable and provide camaraderie, good mental stimulation and exercise. To continue…

I hope you enjoy this book as much as we enjoyed the walks.

David.

Walk 1. Derby to Belper.

The journey begins; this is the first walk of our new adventure. We start by walking past the Brunswick, David's local, to reflect on old times when we walked quite long distances and were quite looking forward to doing it all over again – we discovered that our fitness levels would prove otherwise!

We duly assembled at Derby station, having got up at some ridiculous hour to catch trains and meet connections.

The route was to be a simple one; to follow much of the Derwent Valley Heritage Way (DVH Way) from the Silk Mill, along the river to Belper.

From the station, we walked past the Brunswick Arms – a microbrewery and taphouse; good beer, good food, good company. An historic inn that was opened in 1842 as the Brunswick Railway and Commercial Inn. It is the first purpose-built inn for the use of railwaymen and second-class passengers.

The Brunswick.

Then across the city, dodging traffic attacking us from all angles; cathedral on the left and down to the river by Derby Silk Mill; now also the Derby Industrial Museum.

Derby Silk Mill.

The Silk Mill is the southern end of the World Heritage Site and marks the start of our walk to Malton.

This is the world's first factory built in 1721 and was owned by the Lombe brothers who travelled to Italy to steal the secrets of weaving silk; the style is supposedly based on Italian architecture despite being destroyed twice by fire. This mill marked the start of the Industrial Revolution.

Under the bridge.

Past the Darley Abbey weir.

The walk follows the river to Darley Abbey and a significant weir where we cross the river beside a redeveloped mill to seek out the path over to the left, across fields where the river meanders and there is a great deal of wild life and a large reserve.

There is little to report here the walk is pleasant, flat, well marked and emerges at the A38 by a railway line.

A walk on metalled roads to Long Eaton; a bit of fumbling to find our way and back to the river with a signpost to confirm we'd got our directions right.

Yes, we're on the right path.

From the river, back on to the road to Makeney; feet beginning to feel a bit sore by this stage but thankfully a fairly grassy path round the top of Milford, past a couple of farms and then on the streets of Belper.

Belper is one of those places you hear of but don't go to; it's actually worth the visit. After asking the way we found the bus stop back into Derby. This is where our next walk would start.

In the pub.

Back to Derby, and the Brunswick something to eat and a pint. A very enjoyable day (despite sore feet) and a decision to more fully document the walks so, hopefully, the prose and the whimsy might improve. It was here in the pub that we eventually acknowledged that we are not as young and fit as we used to be and, being old and knackered, to not be so ambitious next time.

On the next walk we learn about way-markers – those signs that indicate the routes of the various heritage trails.

Walk 2. Belper to Whatstandwell.

And Crich Tramway Village.

We make the usual detour, Steve falls over and we visit the tram museum at Crich.

6 O'-Bloody-Clock, thankfully the clocks went back and there's some daylight (but not much). We got together in Derby to start the day with excellent bacon sandwiches which, with a cup of station coffee, passed the time well and gave us time to check bus and rail times.

We caught the bus to Belper using our bus passes to get off at the stop we had used to catch the bus back from the previous walk – so no gaps there. Still enjoyed the 'feel' of Belper as we searched for the start point for this next leg of the journey.

Lots of history, we passed the mill workers' cottages, over the railway to Belper Bridge and one enormous mill on the right.

Belper East Mill.

An information board gives its history. Very impressive building with the horseshoe weir and a small island with mature trees in the middle – how do they manage with drowned roots?

Horseshoe shaped weir.

The view up the Derwent is brilliant and sets the tone for the next mile or so. We followed the lane next to the millworkers' cottages. Through a squeeze stile and along Wyver Lane, which passes a nature reserve – do not enter – where the sign board describes all manner of exotic birds and to prove the point, there's a hide to watch them.

Across the fields, looking out for the yellow waymarks affixed to the stiles that showed where to go next. It got a bit steep here, and we hadn't seen a waymark for some time so senses were heightened as we looked for the next one. We walked parallel to the edge of a wood.

Looking up the Derwent.

And there – over to the right and half-way along the wall, there it was; so, with Steve leading fearlessly forward we got almost to the wall to realise the waymarker was a daffodil! Later we saw several bunches of waymarkers growing along the path and in the shadow of the dry-stone walls.

One of our themes was the regular recognition of way-markers and daffodils. Steve eventually learned to tell the difference!

We followed the Derwent Valley Heritage Way as far as Ambergate and decided it was time for a sit-down and a short break so stopped for coffee and lemonade in The Hurt Arms, a very good pub with a delightful barmaid, who pointed out the route to Crich and the Tram Museum.

The route took us along the Cromford Canal, now well silted but very calm and peaceful, good to be at one with nature. So, along the canal, over the bridge and up the hill through the woods.

Cromford Canal (picture added from a later walk).

At this point we remembered the three of us were Queen's Scouts with badges for hiking, map reading and pioneering amongst other things – and we still had trouble with the scale of the map at 2½ inches to the mile. Regularly readjusting where we thought we were using features from the surrounding countryside.

And wow – was this steep up through these woods!

And muddy; Steve's boots – which have been a bane – gave way at this point and, encouraged by his rucksack, he tumbled over backwards; thankfully steadied by David and on the way over his mind sped up enough to work out the best way to land to avoid rolling right the way back down the hill. Pity his mind doesn't work quite so fast the rest of the time.

Ego bruised and thankfully little else; dusted off and now zig-zagged to the path by the wall at the top which is a boundary to a wood called Bowmer Rough – quite appropriate.

Despite our Queen Scout capabilities, there was a degree of uncertainty about which path to take but there were tyre tracks and signs of other people that led to a corner in a wall, blocked to a height of about six feet.

No idea how the (motor?) cyclists got their vehicles over here, but full marks for determination.

It took each of us about three goes to get on top of the wall and the help of the other two to land on the other side with a degree of safety, upright and with joints intact.

There were similar (motor?) cycle tracks on the other side – profound admiration on our part for the rider.

The path led to an underground reservoir where we discussed the fun and advantages of underground yachting – sheltered from the rain, no dangerous leaning over, no unpleasant jibing …

This reservoir had a sign overlooking the road but no writing on the side facing us, so no clue as to its name.

However, there was a road just through the gate we should be able to better work out where we were; a hundred yards down the road – no help; a hundred yards up the road and we found out the reservoir is called Chadwick Nick (good name for a racehorse or a greyhound?) and importantly, shown on the map.

Crich Tramway Village.

Bearings found – and a signpost (always helpful) and now we should be able to find Crich which is at the top of a hill and houses the national tram museum – Tramway Village.

The entrance to the museum is a long walk from the road, the easy way having been closed off.

We duly bought our entrance tickets, turned them into Gift Aid and were presented with an old penny which is the price of your tram ticket.

The entrance – quite a long way from the road.

14

We then did all the expected things: explored the tram shed, took pictures, and were engaged by some of the oddities – a steam tram, a device for fixing overhead wires, a tram with a built-in turntable and lots more odd and interesting examples of Victorian engineering.

Trams.

The bits most remembered from childhood are: the way the seat backs are devised so that you could sit always facing the front, the narrow winding stair to the upper deck – a real trial for 'larger people'; and days out in Leeds with a tram ride to Temple Newsam, past the Grand Arcade with the clock which had little figures emerge to circumnavigate it and strike bells on the hour to remind us that 'time and tide wait for no man'.

To go with the trams were reminders of days gone by – tile fronted pubs, toilets, phone boxes and undrinkable tea in the terminus café.

A tile fronted pub – and Stingo!!!

Not only in Paris – did the French steal the idea?

And only missing Doctor Who.

A brilliant diversion, evocative memories and tea that tasted like something out of a weasel. It was here we decided this digression was such a good idea that we would try to introduce something of interest to each walk – museums, castles, places you go for a day out – after all, the idea is to get fresh air, see new things and enjoy good company; not to knock ourselves out with a forced march.

So now, our destination was to be the station at Whatstandwell, ideally, stopping at the pub marked on the map for a soothing libation before we caught the train or bus back to Derby.

Out of the museum, turned right and down the hill; sadly, we didn't look closely enough at the 2½ inch map and should have turned left.

After a little while (well quite a long while really) we looked up at a bus stop and realised we had made a detour towards Holloway, so we got the map out again.

Another decision; reduce the planned walk length because every walk so far has involved a bit of dodgy map reading and an interesting detour (remember the earlier comments about expert Queen's Scout map readers!). Now we had our bearings we could head back to Whatstandwell station and Derby.

Down a delightful little path – straight out of Dickens, with interesting houses, cobbles and no room for motor cars, to the lower (Leashaw) road, past some quite smart houses, horses and a (dressage?) arena; lots of 'no entries' and a good number of paths up to the road we had walked down to get to Holloway.

Getting close to the station there's a track down to the Cromford Canal – the one we started from after directions from the delightful barmaid.

As good as the earlier bit – serene, peaceful, magic, a really welcome addition to the walk.

And a pub within striking distance.

Sod. The pub is now a rose-encircled, jam-and-scones tearoom, but with a bus stop so we checked bus times and it would seem they are so frequent people turn out to wave as they come by.

On to the station, ticket machine working, guard a colleague of David, good banter, sunshine and back to Derby.

<u>In the pub.</u>

David's local again; excellent beer – well it should be, coming direct from the attached brewery.

It was in the pub that we twigged that to avoid making the same mistake again it might be helpful to re-learn a bit of botany and what a daffodil looks like.

The next leg of the journey was to be by way of the National Stone Centre – could anything be more thrilling?

Walk 3. Wirksworth, to Whatstandwell.

And the Ecclesbourne Valley Railway.
And the National Stone Centre.

It's 1ˢᵗ August – Yorkshire day, a day in which we take the walk in reverse, take a three mile detour just to get started, ride a restored railway, look at some stones, avoid a storm, see some serious industrial history, talk bollocks (as usual) and fail to get too lost.

All our trains were running to time; met up in Derby where David had produced some bacon rolls that were very welcome, and very tasty; just enough time to finish these treats when the train came to take us from Derby to Duffield and on to the heritage railway (our first bit of culture).

Both Dave and David had made the effort; David with a big white rose on his rucksack; Dave with badges and ancient proclamations.

We had wondered what had happened historically on Yorkshire Day and speculated that the senior Panjandrum (the one with the big flat cap) from each of the Ridings arrived in York at the appointed hour to begin the ceremony, led by the High Muckamuck – he who ran York and had the biggest flat cap of all.

The four officials would migrate from city gate to city gate and at each gate would solemnly proclaim:

"I [insert name here], being a resident of the [insert compass point here] Riding of Yorkshire declare:

That Yorkshire is three Ridings and the City of York, with these boundaries and 1142 years standing;

That the address of all places in these Ridings is Yorkshire;

That all persons born therein or resident therein and loyal to the Ridings are Yorkshire men and women;

That any person or corporate body which deliberately ignores or denies the aforementioned shall forfeit all claim to Yorkshire status.

These declarations on Yorkshire Day 2017.

God Save The Queen".

After this we're not sure what happens, but if Yorkshire tradition and culture is anything to go by, they will head for the nearest pub, grumble and moan for the rest of the afternoon and get pissed on someone else's money.

Now, after this short diversion (unusually, the only one of the day), back to the walk.

Ecclesbourne Valley Railway.

Normally, we would walk from Whatstandwell to Wirksworth but David had cleverly spotted that this would involve a significant amount of up-hill, especially around Cromford and by taking the walk backwards we would have an easier day. In hindsight, this was probably a good thing.

We caught the train to Duffield which is the start of the Ecclesbourne Valley Railway (EVR); run by volunteers and bringing back a host of memories from when as boy scouts we would catch trains like this to go away for a week or so camping with like-minded youngsters, and a long way away from the parents.

The EVR ticket office was well presented, modern print-as-you-go machine and a complete absence of inane literature; just good stuff with places of interest etc.

Ecclesbourne Valley Heritage Railway.

The first stop is Shottle, then through Idridgehay and finally Wirksworth (where do they get these names from?); very impressed with Wirksworth; the quality of the buildings; their architecture and sheer *solidity* which seems to reflect the local stone and quarrying.

And on to an unexpected treat – the National Stone Centre; it's a museum to stone and some of the things you can do with it. The entrances are marked by 'follies' which are presumably test pieces for pupils.

Millennium wall at the National Stone Centre.

The training courses on stone masonry and dry-stone walling were filled for the rest of the year, bar one space on the dry-stone walling course; so still a lot of interest in the old crafts.

Sadly, we didn't have enough time to make the most of the 50 acre site with fossils, features and examples of dry stone walls from around the UK – it is nothing like as boring as it sounds.

Then the rain started and we headed for the café: semi-precious gems, fossils, geological maps and even a seismograph plus a good cup of proper tea and a stunning view through the picture windows. Well worth a second visit when the sun shines.

The rain has now stopped and time to press on, so up the hill to get on to the High Peak Trail; the local map-in-a-frame wasn't too helpful though:

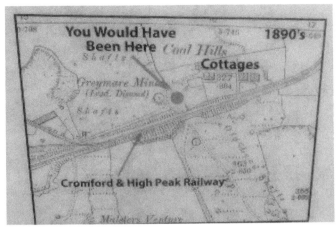

An unhelpful map.

Somehow we muddled through and unexpectedly we found a second Heritage Railway, The Steeple Grange Light Railway which is an 18 inch gauge and originally operated along much of the High Peak Trail; sadly, not operating on the day we visited but is in action on weekends.

On to the High Peak Trail – one where we shouldn't get lost as it's an old railway line; thankfully flat and easy to follow.

There is some very pleasant walking and also things we didn't quite understand like this stile going nowhere:

What is the purpose of this stile?

An area that is cared for as part of the Peak District National Park and largely unspoiled with protection for rare species that is respected:

Protection of rare species.

It was at this scree slope that we calculated the day's timescale was a bit challenging and a bit unclear so we decided not to go to Matlock Bath and to head directly to Cromford. Matlock Bath won't run away and can be saved for next time.

We followed the wall that's up the hill for a bit although the path isn't too obvious and there's quite a lot of mud.

At this point, one of us asked the question "Is it thunder?" and got the answer "No, it's Tuethder". The weather was beginning to look decidedly interesting, we were severely exposed and in the middle of nowhere.

Thunder clouds over Cromford.

We could see odd flashes of lightning and heard quite a lot of thunder; in fact, Dave's wife rang from Sheffield to check we were not caught in the weather.

Subsequently we found out that the storm was fierce enough to flood through part of the Norton library roof – something that has never happened before.

Most of the storm passed north of us, possibly soaking Matlock? A good job we weren't on the Selby to Malton bit today which was atrocious.

As we dropped down through Cromford a number of people (mostly with dogs!) suggested that if we wanted some shelter to move a bit smartish – they live there, know the weather and the limited shelter.

Down a quite steep hill (hate to take a driving test here), past some quite wide streets and stone-built houses.

We passed a significant bus shelter as the weather got a bit ominous it was suggested we might rest here and enjoy our packed lunches; however, on mature reflection it was obvious that there was no chance of rain and so we pressed on.

Sure enough, after a few minutes, big drops getting bigger as we arrived at Cromford Mill which had been built to spin cotton – this will make another good day out when the sun shines.

Cromford Mill.

This is technically the point where the walk should have started, but the heritage railway and Stone Centre were too interesting to miss.

From Cromford Mill it's a short downhill to the canal basin that is the start of the Cromford canal towpath which will take us back to Whatstandwell where we finished the earlier walk.

Luckily there's a cafeteria at the canal basin, so instead of packed lunches we had oven-baked potatoes – a rare treat and under the big umbrellas out of the weather.

The rain passed, heading north through Sheffield to Malton; we were left with odd spots of rain, desultory showers and the threat of something worse that never quite materialised but rain jackets were on and off like a Donald Trump appointment.

We knew that there was a train from Whatstandwell back to Derby at ten to the hour and we had about 55 minutes to catch it.

The station is three miles away (it says here) and to see three senile delinquents yomping along a tow path is not the most edifying of sights; yomp, yomp, yomp; past the sewerage works – quite a distinctive aroma, and through the canal's Gregory tunnel which thankfully has a sound handrail and has a reasonably level walkway – but no lights!

Exiting the tunnel, it was quite noticeable how quiet and peaceful the countryside is at this point, especially after the noise of three old blokes stamping and wheezing along the confined space in the tunnel.

We paused for breath (deep ones) next to the Grade II listed Leawood Pump, an engine house, which was built in 1849 to pump water up from the river Derwent and into the canal. It still operates during weekday afternoons.

The Leawood Pump House – lots of wheezing (us!)

24

And on and on yomping towards Whatstandwell when we passed under a bridge that looked familiar from our earlier descent from Holloway, so a pause, a glance at the map and a breather; meanwhile the clock is still ticking.

There were some superb blackberries over the other side of the canal but out of reach (even if hanging on to each other's coat tails).

The worn stairs to the road running over the bridge, turned out to be someone's back yard, so not as familiar as we thought.

Yomp, yomp. Senior yomping. Slower than teenage yomping when we managed 5 miles in well under the hour with full rucksacks from Helwith Bridge to Settle to catch the last (and only) bus that day back to Bradford. Ah! Memories.

Another milepost that told us we had another mile to go – how long are the soddin' miles round here? And a look at the clock said we wouldn't make it.

But just in case, we decide to press on and if we're overtaken by a train on the railway line below, we can then slow down.

We were overtaken by the train.

So, no need to panic any more, just enjoy the stroll and serenity with an hour or so left for the last quarter mile – and we still have packed lunches to enjoy while we wait for the next train due in an hour or so.

Serenity – we slow down here.

Train arrives, back to Derby and into the pub (not The Brunswick this time).

In the Pub.

A pint – at last! This was the most amazing pint of John Smith on the planet, more like a stout than a bright see-through beer but we were assured (perhaps a little too eagerly) that it <u>really</u> was the proper thing.

In order to escape tomorrow's likely ramifications of this 'John Smiths' our next round a drop of Blond Witch (not Natalie who served us) – delightful, except it's from Lancashire (maybe we ought to look a bit closely at our Yorkshire visas).

So, what had we learned? Other than our level of fitness; that stones can actually be very interesting and that there are something like 24 different ways to construct a dry stone wall. It was a pity that we didn't have longer to spend at the National Stone Centre.

Walk 4. Around Matlock.

And the Heights of Abraham.

A day in which we encountered some quite steep hills, walked along a ledge half way up a precipice, thought we might have taken the customary wrong turn but probably hadn't, took a ride in a cable car and saw a kestrel.

The day was warm and sunny, train timetables a bit of a mystery (so we got together earlier than usual), the harvest is coming in nicely although yields are a bit down because of the dry weather; still harvesting although it was Lammas last week.

The day started in Chesterfield with a walk past the Church with the twisted spire (excellent view of it) from the rail station to the bus station which is tucked away and hard to find (follow the pedestrian signs to the disabled toilet).

We caught the X17 to Matlock and despite being an Xpress service our bus passes were accepted. The scenery is stunning in this part of the world, but quite challenging for traffic as well as people; quite a number of hills at 14% or steeper and traffic jammed up coming into Matlock.

Chesterfield's crooked spire.

Matlock is a significant tourist destination with all the attributes of a thriving community – football team, cricket, bowls, tennis, playgrounds for the kids and large, open public parks – but with a 1930s road system. No wonder the traffic jams up and parking is difficult.

Parking in Matlock.
(can be tricky).

The walk begins in Hall Leys Park and follows the river to the second footbridge, by a green pumping station after passing the miniature railway, where we learned that a *Gricer* is a railway enthusiast; but David knew that anyway.

Matlock's miniature railway.

Over the bridge we turned right (back on ourselves which felt a bit strange) under overhanging rocks that would be a challenge to

climb, until we were in sight of a railway bridge. The path forked –
one fork under the railway, the other upwards – like so many of the
paths we would encounter today.

Railway bridge on the right, fork left.

The upward fork led to the Pic Tor which 'houses' the war
memorial and provides excellent views of Riber castle.

The war memorial and some of the names.

And Riber Castle.

A walk down from the war memorial (downhill at last) when the path forked and we re-joined the original concreted path which took us uphill again (what a surprise!)

A concreted path – uphill naturally.

Our next landmark was a sign behind us over a gate which read *High Tor Grounds*.

The path is a Victorian flint road going upwards with Matlock getting ever smaller below us down a vertical rock face; lots of signs about the inadvisability of leaning over to get a better view.

Yes – that's the one.

Keep going up – and up – and up – and up out of the high-hedges path and into sunlight by a broad viewing point; magnificent. Rest for a while and then bear leftish (no other way) towards the top of High Tor.

Matlock now quite some distance below.

A little further on there are a couple of benches in the shade of a tree. We took the time to stop, relax, enjoy the view and have lunch; some of the smallest pork pies ever manufactured; nice though; and another good view of Riber castle.

Dave (the one with the sharp eyes) pointed to a kestrel that had been watching us all the time, maybe hoping for a piece of pie; its mate emerged from somewhere and they evidently decided to leave us alone.

Badly taken pictures of a kestrel.

Having finished lunch and rested we walked the few yards to the top of High Tor, ready for the descent into the valley and the Heights of Abraham.

The path is a monster for anyone suffering vertigo or slippery feet – a bit like those photos of Chinese monks heading for their mountain-top monastery. It's a few hundred feet straight up and a few hundred yards straight down. The straight up bit bothered us a great deal less than the straight down bit.

The view is brilliant and some thoughtful people have thankfully fixed hand-holds (of sorts) to the rock face for the trickier parts.

The path – one of the easier bits!

And so on down where we thought we had made a wrong turning but probably hadn't[1] so returned, to reach the road a little confused; thankfully a kind gentleman walking his dogs appeared and put us right. Keep going to the White Lion and then take the path to the right. Along the path there is a sign remarkably like the one we had been looking for earlier:

This is possibly where we would have emerged, had we taken the 'wrong turn' and persevered.

The Heights of Abraham.

A little further down we came to the entrance for the cable car to the summit of the Heights of Abraham; it has been a long time since any of us had taken a cable car, so this was a bit of a treat.

-----

[1] A bit like the politician's apology 'I thought I made a mistake but I was wrong'. Goes with 'lessons have been learned'.

A gondola.

Well worth the visit, a surprisingly good cup of tea and a host of attractions; we didn't do much with the attractions other than look at various fossils and minerals.

A look at the time and the bus timetable when we decided we'd better get away if we were to enjoy some beer together before we went our different ways; so back down the cable car, noticing on the other side of the valley the twisting the rock had gone though in geological time.

Now back along the river towards Matlock; the dry weather has left the river really low when it is normally active enough to support a canoe slalom course.

This should be a torrent.

We walked back to Matlock bus station, passing through a number of little parks along the riverside, in one of which we had lunch. Then the bus back to Chesterfield.

In the pub.

The Rectory pub served a very welcome pint, some interesting things with chips, and space to reflect on what we had accomplished during such a hot day: only six miles, but the heat and exertion up those hills made it feel like ten (smug smile).

What we learned is that it's quite steep around Matlock and a bit daunting for the faint hearted.

We'll be planning soon for the bit that's missing from Matlock to Cromford Mill (a day of culture in the offing – noted at the end as walk $4^1/_2$).

And a sunset.

Walk 5. Baslow to Matlock.

November 2018 – supposed to be sunny.

A longish walk which where we followed the Derwent downstream from Chatsworth House, saw the deer and the big fountain; got drizzled on near an old Church, contemplated fishing, gained a free pint, saw quite a variety of different cloud types and did really well with our timing.

We arrived behind schedule in Chesterfield, which has now become a bit of a start point; the train was running late due to a suicide near Newcastle, and on disembarking we were 'beset' by the Samaritans trying to reduce rail suicides.

The Samaritans took one look at the three of us and immediately gave David a 'get in touch' card – can't understand why.

Coffee, chat to the Samaritans and off for the bus. Despite the lateness David had left plenty of time to walk to the bus stop; yet having visited Chesterfield on several occasions, Steve still has no idea where the bus stop is but, thankfully, he had two competent guides.

Onto the 170 bus; Bus Passes at the ready, Dave's fired up on the third attempt. Through striking countryside and some very posh houses into Baslow to get off by the green and search around for the start of the walk.

The start to the walk is the path next to the coffee shop, by the side of the thatched cottages.

The clouds were quite dramatic at times, with the first of the formations looking like upside-down sand dunes, complete with the little trickles of sand.

Upside-down dunes (Mackerel?)

The start of the walk.

Through a fancy kissing gate which is actually more like a revolving door, designed for visitors to Chatsworth who need a wheelchair – great idea and very thoughtful.

The lads behind bars – and a good thing at that.

THE CANNON KISSING GATE
GIVING ACCESS TO THE PARK
FOR VISITORS IN WHEELCHAIRS,
WAS INSPIRED BY MRS. JILL CANNON,
MADE AND DONATED BY MATHERS ENGINEERING
OF TIBSHELF AND OPENED BY THE DUKE OF
DEVONSHIRE AND MRS. CANNON ON THE
17th MARCH 1999

The path leads through the deer park; wide open spaces, peaceful, with few people, no yapping dogs and a clear sky with wisps of cloud and quite a distance to the big house – hardly surprising the gentry were all good at riding horses.

The White Lodge.

The path divides by the White Lodge, one track heading to Chatsworth, the other more-or-less straight on to meet the river Derwent.

And more or less straight on.

Chatsworth House is now big enough to see, with its Emperor Fountain to one side. There were marquees and walkways over the grass in preparation for Friday's start to *Christmas at Chatsworth* – over 100 stalls with lots to choose from.

Preparing for Christmas.
Fountain in the background and a draughty top floor.

It was about this point that Dave reminded Steve that this is a deer park and there are actually deer roaming freely; this had been overlooked in contemplating what a rotten night's sleep a visitor would get staying in the draughty top floor of the North Wing.

Deer!

Onwards and upwards, contemplating the fountain and how it got to push water so high – the reservoir behind the trees which has some sort of minor fortification, looking quite impressive amongst the remaining autumn colours.

Imposing tower of unknown purpose.

39

More clouds, those on the right look like five small fishes. (Mackerel?)

Follow the river to Queen Anne's Bower which looks impressive at first except the moat is only two feet deep and the terrace on top is boring and covered in grass and weeds.

Chatsworth House, North Wing, Tower & Fountain.

Leaving Chatsworth behind – the grounds are immense and took a fair part of the walk – we followed the river and turned right by the old ruined corn mill and upwards towards the road.

Approaching the ruined corn mill.

Across the road and into the car park, past the garden centre and tea rooms – it's a longish walk today, so not enough time to linger; the path bears to the right by a saw mill, past two cottages and then a sharp left through Carlton Lees.

Tree that's seen better days.

A signpost by a stile points us towards Rowsley and through fields of cows of indeterminate temper – but definitely in charge and on their own territory. A bit of respect is called for here.

Cattle & autumn colours.

The path follows the river, and so did we, to make the obligatory detour having missed the stile (with obvious way marker) half way along the other side of the field.

From here, for the next mile or so to Rowsley was quite boggy and sad; good job the boots were waterproof and we have had practice in slipping and falling over; so managed to stay upright.

Mud.

More mud.

Through the (muddy) railway arch, past farm buildings, more mud and into the village of Rowsley.

A walk to the main road (A6), with the Peacock Hotel on the junction, turn left, over the bridge, past the Grouse & Claret, past the *Peak Shopping Village* and into Old Station Close which is a small (and a bit muddy) industrial estate.

At the back of the industrial estate is a walk through to the concrete path that leads over a plastic bridge and, eventually, to the narrow-gauge railway.

Plastic bridge looking forward.

Plastic bridge looking backward.

It's quite long and boring – but easily maintained.

The path, which is quite enclosed, leads past the civic amenities (that's a municipal tip to you and me) and then out and into the road.

After our usual bit of confusion (not helped by a friendly cyclist) we walked to the heritage railway which only runs on Saturdays and Sundays this time of year with the last train in November last Sunday (so a long wait for the next one – a bit like the modern railway timetable).

Heritage railway, sign could do with some TLC.

At the end of the tracks the path continues through a squeeze stile and along the river Derwent.

A Tranquil River Derwent.

And now into more fields littered with sheep (although signed as cows) with a broad track and a longish walk past the farmhouse.

A bit strange to see cherry blossom this time of year.

On into Churchtown with St. Helen's Church founded about 900 AD and open to all (sadly locked!), but which has a bench in the graveyard where we decided to enjoy a somewhat late lunch.

St. Helen's Church.

With several old coffin (sarcophagus?) lids in the porch that was locked.

It rained at this point, so waterproofs out and a grumble at Carol whose weather forecast at 7:00 this morning had promised a lovely day. Earlier we had noticed a *mackerel sky* and ignored the country saying "Mackerel sky, mackerel sky, not long wet, not long dry".

It brightened up soon after, though.

Out of the Churchyard there's a signpost and a gate down the side of the graveyard; this is the start of the next part of the journey which follows a muddy beck, past the cricket ground and onto a road where we turned right past the caravans to the Square & Compass.

Kids making good use of bits of road cones to fashion a swing.

Square & Compass.

Darley Bridge is the next landmark, signed by a box of plants with the pansies and others making a great display (odd at this time of year).

Over the bridge, following the very obvious sign to Oaker (Gated road) and along the river (still tranquil).

Another tranquil river.

It was around here that memories of an old school friend emerged who was a very keen fisherman, whether with bait, lure or flies and the thought of a few quiet hours, bottle of beer keeping cool in the stream; and don't bother with the bait; seemed like a very attractive way of spending an afternoon all to yourself.

The plants had been quite fascinating with flowers emerging out of season. Additionally, we were used to seeing apples being picked from trees rampant with foliage, but here the apples were in the nude. We don't have a resident *malologist* but this did seem a bit odd.

Apples in the nude.

The broad, easy track continues through the village of Oaker; where, a short way into the village there's an obvious signpost to the left indicating a public footpath. We turned down here back to the river and a distant view of Riber Castle.

The riverside path boasts a railing down one side which seems to last for ever, at one point passing alongside a significant derelict works.

The everlasting path.

The path eventually opens out a bit and passes beneath a station. At this stage it seemed that Dave had sped up a bit (well we were nearing the end). We walked (yomped?) alongside a steel railway bridge, under a stone railway bridge, back alongside an embankment and discovered 'civilisation' on the other side of the river.

'Civilisation'(?)

And then *pop!* We emerged in Matlock, just as it was getting dark – brilliant timing.

The bus back to Chesterfield was due out in just a few minutes and we were prepared to spend an hour in Matlock waiting for the next one, but traffic is heavy and we had yomped the last bit so decided to see if there was a chance of catching the bus – made it with two minutes to spare – brilliant timing.

<u>In the pub.</u>

Back in Chesterfield a meal and a free pint at the Burlington then off to the train. We had learned that by getting our timing right the day had come together better than ever before – and it continued:

The express to Edinburgh got stuck behind a slow train, 25 minutes late; Steve's train was running just late enough to make the connection with three minutes to spare – brilliant timing.

A brilliant day.

And some left-over photos.

Clouds.

More clouds.

Fountain amongst the autumn at Chatsworth.

Walk 6. Wadshelf to Baslow.

November 2019; Moist (in lumps).

*Weather very different from when we were last here, lots of mud,
sodden fields – some planted. A wood that could be from a film,
badger setts? Quite a lot of road, lunch under some big rocks, the
last bit of our planned footpath was about six inches under water,
beer in Baslow and a long, wet wait for a late-running bus.*

We met in Chesterfield after David (he of the railways) caught the
wrong train; bacon sandwich, coffee and Steve was helped (yet
again) to find the stop for the 170 bus. After an uneventful ride we
landed in Wadshelf, took stock and walked up the hill.

Out of Wadshelf. Must be great view on a sunny day.

Up to the crossroads by the school where a signpost tells us that
it's only four miles to Balsow.

Only four miles – cobblers!

Ignoring the signpost, we walked over the road and up the track by the side of the sign and towards Moorhay Farm. Four miles by road was not enough to make a good walk so we selected a moist route over moorland to provide some interest.

Loads of mud.

And a few dispirited animals.

Past Moorhay Farm the path diverges; the left fork (which we should have taken) leading to Freebirch Farm and the B 6050; the right-hand track led off towards woods, so we took this instead.

By the left!

Possibly due to the weather, or a legal dispute, this path had been diverted, and now went down the side of a garage and into Chaneyfield Wood.

Not quite sure what to expect.

Between the red car and the garage.

English woodland in autumn.

Very pleasant walking through the woods with a small stream (Birley Brook) burbling along below. We emerged by a hedgerow with the farm in the distance and what we guessed were either badger setts or fox holes, but no smell of foxes.

A badger sett?

The path has little of note or any distinguishing features as it runs alongside big fields that have been planted and are beginning to germinate. Emerging by the roadside to see a signpost telling us that Baslow was now three miles away – a mile gained for about two and a half miles walked!

This is the bit where we follow the road for half a mile or so to Cornerstone Farm where Baslow is signed again so we turn right to Balsow along the B6050.

Muddy track – road on the left.

The next couple of miles are on the road, which might have been a blessing in disguise, because it was quite dry underfoot whilst the countryside tracks and fields were all but impassable.

Robin Hood Inn.

A couple of miles easy walking and we're at the Robin Hood Inn, famous enough to be put on the map.

The B6050 merges here with the A619 signposted to Chesterfield (sounds more like a drive than a walk); after a short way we pass the Eric Byrne Campsite and a little way past Eric's driveway there is a path over the other side of a fairly high wall.

And over the wall (is it a stile, a ladder or what?)

The path is an easy moorland walk, past an enclosure, through dried bracken and a few jumbled rocks; we aimed for a big lump of rock called the *Three Men*.

Easy moorland walk; Three Men rocks at top right.

By now, we had been walking for quite some time and were due for lunch. The *Three Men* seemed like a good place to stop.

Eventually, we found a spot out of the wind and missed by most of the drizzle. Damp sandwiches and a view that would be brilliant if it wasn't for the mist.

Three Men, our cafeteria, for half an hour or so.

And what should be a brilliant view. Baslow below.

The track from here leads directly to the A621 (Sheffield Road), we were going to follow the track across the road and into Baslow from the western approaches; but, looking over the wall at the flowing path, decided that discretion was the better part of valour, abandoned the idea of a walk along a streaming country trail, got back on the road again and directly into Baslow.

Path somewhere down there.

A check on the bus schedule and we had quite a long wait.

<u>In the pub.</u>

Plenty of time for a couple of pints in the Devonshire Arms and then to the bus stop with ten or so minutes to spare. We had learned that there is no shame in making a diversion when the alternative is ankle-deep water and mud.

Finished our beer and out to the bus-stop. No bus, sodding thing had been held up and we waited (fairly) patently in the cold and damp for about three quarters of an hour. Took one look at the driver's face and decided any humour was out of the question.

Back to Chesterfield and home – a bit late and still a bit moist.

Walk 7. Wadshelf to Chesterfield.

June 2019; a really nice day – between storms.

Very English clouds, meadows, meadows, meadows, a bit of mowing, took the wrong turning (great walk though) and surprised with the extent of the country walks and greenery coming back into Chesterfield.

We met in Chesterfield where Steve still hasn't learned to navigate to the bus stop despite several earlier expeditions around the town. With bus passes at the ready we're onto the 170 bus to Wadshelf. A bus with about 85% grey hairs.

Very English clouds over Chesterfield.

Through the stone cottage village of Old Brompton, through Wigley (which we will see again later) to Wadshelf. Disembark, check the map and away we go down Netherfield Lane, past lots of plants in bloom and a Victorian Post Box which looks like it's still operational.

The start of the walk is clearly marked and takes us across the first of many meadows with stunning views over the moors. This was to be a day of walking over endless meadows, long grass and wild flowers; occasionally disturbing the odd grouse or pheasant.

The start of a very pleasant day.

After the wet and misery of earlier months the fields have now transformed from mud and puddles into lush crops apparently growing well and thickly, such that the path for the first half of the journey (to the Linacre Reservoirs) could be quite hard to spot.

There's a path here somewhere.

Over meadows and through dappled woodland we emerged to turn right – our first, but quite minor, detour.

"Hey David, there's a stream here that should be somewhere else. Do you think we should look at the map again?"

So, back on ourselves, up the hill over the meadow walking now towards Wigley; emerging by The Royal Oak.

The Royal Oak.

The map indicates that if we turn right here there will be a path to the left which will lead to the reservoirs; sure enough – a *Footpath* sign, so off we went, down a hole and into a meadow.

Down a hole and off to the meadow.

Usual difficulty finding our way over various walls or through gates, but perseverance paid off and, having walked all the way round a field set up for horse jumping, we found a gate tied shut with string.

Gate; note footpath near right-hand gate-post.

After a bit more casting around we found the path and a little way along the path the landowner had kindly mowed it for us, so at last, easy navigation.

From this ...

... to this.

The only slight problem was that the easy navigation took us over more meadows – but to the wrong spot; where we could overlook the reservoir, but not get down to it.

Great view though!

Linacre Reservoir; superb view.

So, we continued on, following the mowed path around more meadows, back over several stiles with holes cut below for the dog to get through (if we had a dog), back past the same field set up for horse jumping where we walked earlier, back through the gate tied with string and back up the hole to the main road.

Time to reconsider; after a bit of advanced map-reading (Dave's satnav app on his posh phone) we decided to continue along the road on the basis we had been a bit previous in following the first footpath sign we came to; and, sure enough after about half a mile there is a second sign, also not very obvious.

A second footpath.

Alongside the building, into a meadow, through a gate, into another meadow, through a gate, jink left and right through a gate and into yet another meadow. Easy going and the views and smells were amazing.

We were now overlooking the reservoir from a different point with an obvious path leading to it.

To the left on the edge of a field, all on its own is a bench big enough for two people (Steve's buttock went numb from sitting on the arm), so we enjoyed lunch with another great view of the reservoir.

Our lunch-time view.

All manner of wild plants; David had brought his book so, with some authority, we could see there were buttercups, clover of many colours, daisies and fieldmouse ear (or is it Field mouse-ear?) We also heard a skylark.

This was the point when we began to notice the dogs, (why were they mainly spaniels?), being taken for walks and emerging from the corner of the field along the path we were about to take past the reservoir.

Setting off again (tricky getting the knees to work again, as well as Steve's buttock) we got coated in pawmarks and saliva (those spaniels again) on the way through a wood to the first reservoir's dam.

And along the dam.
A couple of seconds after the grebe had dived!

The walk back into Chesterfield from here is along wide, well-maintained paths that emerge at the edge of the town which might explain the number of dogs being walked.

There are quite a number of educational and decorative carvings which add to the walk:

Educational.

And Decorative.

From this point on, there is little to report that hasn't already been said; the broad track took us past a ranger station where the toilets added a bit of gentility to the usual tree or hedge.

Waiting outside the ranger station for a bus to pick them up (and evidently a bit bored) were a tribe of apprentice hooligans – all of them about seven years old throwing plastic bottles of water around and supervised by a very patient teacher.

The path which carries cycles and dogs as well as walkers continues on through Holmbrook Valley park to some more bridge 'art' – seems there's a lot of it in this part of the world.

Bridge Art. Roy Orbison on the right?

From Holmbrook park we continued through Tapton park along wide, well-marked paths signing the town centre.

Easy to follow signs.

Past an impressive laburnum as we tracked around the side of a large housing estate.

An impressive laburnum.

<u>In the pub.</u>

The first pub we stopped in served either old beer or had unwashed lines; so we decanted to the Pig & Pump – a pub where the bar staff really know their job and the assorted varieties of sausage and mash really hit the spot.

We had learned that the traditional English meadow still exists and is alive and well. This was the perfect place to turn our attention to the next bit of the walk and its timing, so that we could attend the Barrow Hill Beer Festival as our 'cultural diversion'.

Refreshed, replete and still a little bit stiff, it was time to head home with the sun setting behind Eggborough power station – very picturesque.

Picturesque sunset, complete with vapour trails.

Section 2: CHESTERFIELD TO SELBY

This is my section of the walk. Whilst I was brought up in West Riding of Yorkshire, at the age of 18 I absconded to Sheffield for three years at the University. I came to love the 'village' of Sheffield, with its steel mills belching out fumes and smoke, its 'little mesters' doing wonderful things with cutlery and silverware and its people, who had, and still have, a unique sense of humour.

I lived as a student in the east end of the city – the rough end – Sedan Street, to be exact. That gives you some idea of how old the houses were! The area had a wonderful sense of community in the mid 60s and a pride in the houses, with people regularly 'donkey-stoning' the edge of their front steps so that you could see them in the dark. The terrace houses in Sedan Street don't exist now; they are all grassed over. I suspect that the sense of community has faded, too.

Sadly, in 1969 I left Sheffield and Yorkshire, and spent my career trying to live in as many counties as I could (Gloucestershire, Herefordshire, Hertfordshire, Kent, Nottinghamshire, to name just a few) and working in virtually all European and North American countries where I could find work. Like many Yorkshiremen, though, including Steve, I found myself back in Yorkshire – back home. It's fitting, then, that this section of the walk takes us through an area that I know well and now call home; Chesterfield, Sheffield and Doncaster.

Dave.

Walk 8. Chesterfield to Halfway.

And the beer festival (twice).
May 17th 2018 & May 16th 2019.

There's a bit of poetic licence here; we walked from Chesterfield to Halfway, and as a separate walk from Chesterfield as far as Katey's Café and then on to the Barrow Hill Beer Festival. We felt the beer festival was sufficiently cultural to include (twice!).

Lovely mornings both days, blossom, peace, wild garlic, decision about the next long walk, a love of gravy, a beer festival with drink in American 'pints', uneven floors, a 5p profit, grumpy with pubs that stopped serving early, finally a good meal, leisurely trips home, Steve can't remember what he had for dinner.

It was a pleasure to get up early, stroll to the train – instead of the usual canter – have time to sit in the early sun and take stock of what was happening round and about. The coffee from the station café smelt really good.

Sat next to a character in distinctive pork-pie hat, Union Jack socks, bovver boots and a trolley loaded with outdoor-sleeping-rough-for-a-couple-of-days gear. Headed for Windsor and the wedding between Prince Harry and Meghan Markle?

Found a seat and travelled through fields that are now green with the corn sprouting, no longer orange and muddy, the river Derwent was sleepy and lugubrious – and, the hawthorn was in blossom – on time this year.

Uneventful rail journey to meet David on the way in Sheffield and convene by the coffee shop, Dave brought bacon butties and we enjoyed a leisurely start.

The only minor concern was that David had left the maps behind, along with a book and his memory so we depended on autopilot.

Out of the station, turn right onto the road, 50 yards or so there's a bridge over the river, over the bridge and have to turn left because there's a gate the other way and another 50 yards or so we're on the Chesterfield canal.

We had a map, of sorts, and Dave had his satnav app so we checked to see if we had got it right.

Dave looking a bit puzzled.

We had! The next four miles or so were along the canal in lovely weather with the canal calm, the blossom fragrant and the wild garlic in profusion – and smelly.

**The bit where the canal overflows into the river
to maintain the right water level.**

Other than being assailed by cyclists, overweight joggers and dog-walkers the walk seemed to go a lot more quickly than the last time we came here. Perhaps because last time it was grey, drizzly and generally miserable with little emerging in the way of new leaves, chicks and interesting smells.

There's not a lot more to say about a restful, peaceful walk along a canal, so here's a couple of pages of pictures:

An interesting signpost – not many like this.

Sign under a bridge.
– not sure what it's trying to tell us.

There is light at the end of the tunnel.

What a way to spend a Thursday.

Blossom.

And now, to Katey's Café where we enjoyed toasties and tea before taking our lives in our hands on the main road. This was where we decided our next walk (having completed Derby to Malton) would be the length of the Chesterfield Canal (in summer).

Katey's Café, something to eat and then up to the main road.

We digressed at this point to the Rail Ale Festival at Barrow Hill.

Poetic license. An earlier walk had taken us from here to Halfway, continuing along the Cuckoo Way to the Eckington Road bridge where road, rail and path all come together. The narrative now is the continuation of the earlier walk, when the weather had been quite miserable.

A quite standard bridge.

The Cuckoo Way and Trans-Pennine Trail cross at this point and we decamped to the Trans-Pennine Trail which follows the disused Chesterfield Canal, unsurprisingly, it is level and very boring; little to report or comment on, other than our feet were getting a bit sore by here and the weather was quite dismal.

Dull enough to set as an exam.

It seemed interminable and several times we asked 'are we nearly there yet?' There seem to be a number of false finishes.

The Trans-Pennine Trail and the Cuckoo Way eventually re-join and shortly after meet the Sheffield Country Walk. A little further on, there's a road bridge back over the disused canal and the river Rother to cross a park that leads to Halfway.

Really enjoying this!

The path from the park emerges into what feels like a big industrial estate; lots of dead ends, turns and little in the way of signposts. Finally, on to a main road (which we found out later that this is the Rotherham Road). Across a busy roundabout and – Behold the Halfway Interchange.

Tram into Sheffield Centre, some beer and a meal then to the rail and bus stations for home on public transport.

<u>Now to the more interesting bit.</u>

<u>*Barrow Hill Rail Ale Festival (twice).*</u>

From Katey's Café we turned left and up to the road over the canal where, taking our lives in our hands, we followed a winding and narrow busy road to the Barrow Hill Roundhouse, an old engine shed from the days of steam.

An absolutely brilliant display of an unsupported roof, locomotives, turntables and sheer-legs thicker then telegraph poles for lifting engine bodies <u>manually!</u> All run by volunteers who seemed to enjoy getting covered in grease.

And good weather for this cultural (?) diversion.

Greeted by a lovely old loco.

Loco on the original turntable – Note the glitterball in the funnel!

And the rest of the afternoon spent in the sunshine, enjoying various beers that ranged from excellent to "definitely not to our taste", a variety of food tents and actually somewhere to sit. – Bliss.

A bit surprising for a UK festival that the glasses (see above) are American 'pint' glasses which only hold 16 oz. however, the prices had been adjusted accordingly (unlike America) so everything was OK.

And what a setting for a beer festival; the floor must be one of the most uneven in England, but a grand excuse for walking a bit wobbly after a few.

5:00PM ejected, but still with some money on the cards we had bought to get in (and avoid cash at the stands) but we weren't allowed back in and no-one outside was allowed near money. One of the doormen kindly went back into the main setting and, because of a lack of change, we made a 5p profit!

The free bus had been stopped by now so we had to use a service bus (along with a load of grumbly drunkards), so our bus passes were useful. Back into Chesterfield and thought it would be right to take another picture of the famous spire.

So here it is (again).

Decision made – if the weather is as good as this next year Barrow Hill will become an annual pilgrimage.

Train back into Sheffield and to our usual watering-hole, bought beer, only to find the chef had been sent home because of lack of interest. Grumble.

Two other likely pubs – finished serving food. Grumble again.

On to The Graduate. Finally, a good meal but can't remember what it was other than it was really tasty and with a dollop of interesting spicy stuff to accompany it.

And after a relaxing day, time to head back home; trains on time, connections made – couldn't have been better.

Second Rail Ale event and pictures from 2019.

This year volunteers were cleaning up the river and river bank – it looked a lot more cluttered, polluted and loaded with plastic than last time, lots of filled bags and full marks to the organisers.

We soon found a diversion with an almost unintelligible 'helpful' instruction as to how we could continue the walk; after a bit of translation we ascended stone steps that were dangerous even in dry weather.

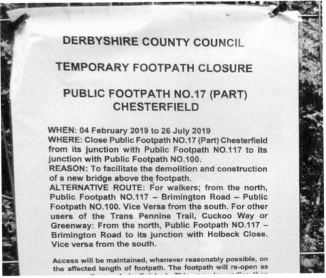

A helpful instruction?

We followed the road for a bit and then descended where it looked right – it was, so back on track and heading for the beer.

The canal hasn't changed much; still hawthorn in blossom and little to add to the previous report other than a couple of families of ducks, wild flowers and the reflections of trees in the canal. Very spring-like and all very satisfying.

Flowers, ducks and reflections.

Stopped again at Katey's Café; lunchtime with pie and mushy peas doused in gravy. The lady running the café appeared with a jug of gravy to ask if we wanted more – they must love the stuff here.

And, again taking our lives in our hands we left the canal-side and walked the short distance to Barrow Hill. We even found a table.

Loco on the turntable (no glitter ball this year).

The steam engines were there with the turntable turning every half hour or so to remind us about the original purpose of the engine shed and all around there are reminders of the quality of riveting and other engineering skills which seem to be dying away.

After an amazing sausage roll and more beer, it was time to head home. The free bus was late so to save time we caught the local service bus and visited a number of housing estates, back lanes and places of no particular interest into Chesterfield.

In the pub.

Some weeks earlier David had been asked to prepare a reference for a past colleague and took us to the Pig & Pump where the reference had been prepared and was very agreeable, so we went back – and it was. Excellent bar staff, a burger with peanut butter and other amazing stuff – called the 'Trust Me' not sure what it was but very good indeed.

We had learned that Barrow Hill is an excellent cultural experience (twice); the only downside was getting used to American 16oz 'pints'.

The next bit is into Sheffield and we pondered on the likelihood of there being any grass or soft bits to walk on, expecting to spend most of the time on paved footpaths.

End of another excellent day, then homeward-bound with the skies clouding over ready for a cooler tomorrow.

Walk 9. Halfway to Sheffield Centre.

A day in which we covered two of the wildlife centres on the outskirts of Sheffield, saw a gap for very thin horses, a useless gate and were quite taken aback by the amount of greenery and nature just off the A57 and Sheffield Parkway.

All met in Sheffield station and then out of the back door to catch the tram to Halfway (good things these bus passes) and a degree of casting around for Station Road which heads east to the Rother Valley Country Park.

The start of the more scenic part of the walk is marked by three sculpted metal hooligans at the top of a slight incline.

Metal hooligans.
Halfway in the distance.

And away we go, along a well-defined path that didn't let us down the entire length of the walk.

And we're off.

We were left in little doubt as to where our path lay and where we were not allowed to walk.

Not sure where the thin ice is though.

And a very tranquil and pleasant walk through the reserve where there is a lot of work nowadays keeping it up to scratch, and with local community involvement. The town of Beighton overlooks Mrs. Minton's Meadow.

The local primary school (Reignhead) helped to create Mrs. Minton's Meadow which is one of the new meadows along the Waterthorpe and Ochre Dyke Wildflower Corridor, not only providing a great place to visit but also teaching the kids about conservation.

As we left the town of Beighton, the path crosses the A57 for the first time.

A fairly quiet A57 – from this.

And then immediately into woodlands and a broad path.

To this.

This path more or less follows the A57 to Shirebrook Nature Reserve and evidently caters for remarkably thin horses and riders.

Wonder how they do it?

And through a nature reserve that we have never heard anyone from Sheffield mention. Are they remarkably lucky but just don't know about it?

Flowers and flying things.

Smelter Wood marks the end of the nature reserve before we meet the A57 again.

Walking over the A57.

And still a bit non-plussed that such a good walk and nature could be had this close to such a busy trunk road.

And then we emerged into open sunlight on the walk down to Sheffield.

A remarkably smug David.
Having read the map correctly (this time).

And a steady walk into Sheffield City Centre, past a couple of famous (or infamous) landmarks.

Park Hill Flats – Grade 2 listed.

We decided on an interesting pint in the brewery that's a short walk from the station, but it was closed – again.

<u>In the pub.</u>

Back to the city centre for a Wetherspoons deal and then home after realising just how much open space there is along a major trunk road.

We learned that Sheffield is the most wooded city in Europe and, unique in the world, with about one third of the city within a national park. We wondered if the next bit to Meadowhall would be as verdant.

And another useless gate.

Walk 10. Sheffield Centre to Meadowhall.

And Kelham Island Museum.

A journey in which the actual mileage involved is not that great so we decided to include a significant dollop of industrial culture in Kelham Island. We walked past where 'the Full Monty' was filmed and followed a nice level canal. It did go on a bit though.

Arrived Sheffield Station, coffee, bacon sandwich, a bit of catching up and out by the front door, past the wall that's a fountain, through the bus station and on to Park Square roundabout which is a sort of maze for trams as they re-route in all directions.

Down the slope is the River Don which constitutes much of the walk and passes Kelham Island where there is a brewery and the industrial museum.

The actual start of the walk.

Kelham Island Museum.

A short distance along the river we meet the Kelham Island Museum which houses some magnificent old static engines, early machinery and memorabilia from the steel and cutlery industries; well worth a visit.

No Dave – it's over there.

The museum is on three floors and includes:

On the ground floor – static engines, heavy industry, armaments and some incredibly mucky light trades (such as knife grinding).

On the first floor is the national fairground archive with some monster puppets, swings we remembered from travelling fairgrounds of years ago and a transport gallery.

And, on the second floor is another transport gallery that overlooks what must be the biggest vice in the world, various things with cogs and work in progress.

This monster has three cylinders – each 40" diameter and 48" stroke, generates 12,000 HP and can be reversed at the flick of a switch – brilliant, but frightening.

A bomb.

And some armour.
(wonder if it worked?)

15' puppets and a fairground swing (front left).

The Boneshaker.

Motorised Transport!

After several hours being impressed by steam (well, compressed air nowadays) and a visit to the past, where we actually remembered some of the stuff, it was back to the walk.

Start of the second part.

As with many of the walks, we quite like level ground and try to make best use of old railways and canals but first we had to follow the river Don for a short way back to where we started.

A wreck and a giant squid – not many of them in Sheffield.

We walked back from Kelham Island to the swing bridge at the Sheffield basin which put us on the canal that goes all the way to Meadowhall.

This is the stretch of water where, in the film, The Full Monty had our hero stood on top of a car that was more or less submerged after the little lad had tipped the steel girder into the canal.

An uneventful start (car now removed).

The canal itself has lots of character and no doubt a selection of characters living by the waterside.

Evidently unhappy with inconsiderate canal users.

We simply followed the towpath with little to report other than remembering where to cross the canal so that we were on the correct side to come off at Meadowhall.

Cross somewhere around here.

Then lots more canal – it probably went on a mile or so further than is reasonable and, unusually, it got a bit boring.

Eventually, we popped up in Meadowhall.

Are we nearly there yet? – Thankfully, Yes.

Once again, we were taken aback by the amount of countryside around one of England's biggest industrial cities.

Sadly, no pub so away home a bit early after an excellent day and lots to look back on.

Walk 11. Meadowhall to Elsecar.

April 9th – between the mist and the rain.

The day we walked from Meadow Hall to Elsecar via Wentworth (not the Berkshire golf course) and didn't get properly lost despite no map and Dave navigating by recipe, fly tipping along the roads, we missed the mist and dodged the rain (just), Dave's ankle stood up well; a number of follies, a mausoleum and some pretty smart park benches.

The weather has been bad for a number of weeks; the bridge in Malton almost submerged but the walk is mainly on roads and hard(ish) ground with a forecast for a day of variable weather and not too cold, so we decided to go for it, even though the distance is slightly longer than we have been used to of late and Dave's broken ankle still had to be tested.

We met at what has become a pretty standard time in Sheffield (10:00 ish) and took the tram to the Meadowhall terminus, which was the bit we had added on from an earlier walk. David was keen to see the new railway lines which will extend the tram route to Rotherham. Can't understand why.

Meadowhall and away we go.

After a bit of fumbling around we found the Ibis Hotel where we had to turn left to walk out of Sheffield alongside the MI and past the crane depots where the cranes sport cheerful Christmas lights and celebratory whatnots; but, before we reached the crane depots we had to walk past a decorative elephant.

A decorative elephant.

The elephant marks the start of many miles of wayside rubbish, fly tipping, bad manners, disregard to the countryside and general pig-ignorance.

Rubbish.

Fly tipping.
A wayside of rubbish and fly tipping – bloody disgrace.

Grumbling over, back to the walk; it was quite salutary to see the cranes close up – they're ever so big and so much spare gantry and tower structure lying around waiting to go and build something. Apparently when a building is complete it's not uncommon to remove the gantries, counterweights and control cabin, leaving the tower behind which then becomes a lift shaft.

Cranes – the ones you can see from the M1.

Some of the kit.

Leaving the cranes behind we walked to where the road passes under the M1 along Grange Lane towards Rotherham until we got to Thundercliffe Grange – what a great name; then along the public right of way across the golf course and some lunch on a bench.

Time for tiffin (ooh posh) – and a great view.

Back to the path and past the clubhouse where the recipe indicated a gentle sweep right which took us past a practice green and up on to the links. It felt a bit odd but thankfully there were a couple of golfers who we could ask the way to the Droppingwell which would take us to the A629 Wortley Road.

Becoming the usual look of puzzlement.

Lots of discussion and then back on Grange Park's main track (the little bit of getting lost mentioned earlier) and on to the A629.

The first of several follies. This one is Keppel's Column which the council won't let you up because it's unsafe, they can't afford to do it up and won't sell it. Perhaps they're waiting for it to fall down and use the land for flats (it already has a building there, so would planning permission be easy?)

95

The day was clouding in a bit and we felt there might be some rain; with it getting humid and jackets becoming a bit sticky up the arms.

Kepple's Column (a folly).

Out through the main gates, turn right and on our way, past a municipal park with some of the snazziest benches we have seen for some time – is there a local councillor with taste?

A decorative bench and the golf club entrance.

Past the Kimberworth Park pub and on to the Milton Arms to turn left along a public footpath with a great view and what we thought was a folly but chatting to a lovely couple from Barnsley, they put us right – it's the Rockingham Monument, designed by John Carr in 1783 as a memorial to the 2nd Marquis of Rockingham. It's open on Sundays. We could only see the top part of the three-storey monument.

It's the Rockingham Monument (not a folly).

The next folly we saw was Hoober Stand, designed by Henry Flitcroft and built by the 1st Marquis of Rockingham in 1747-8 to commemorate the defeat of the Jacobite rebellion.

Tastefully converted windmill? No, Hoober Stand.

Onwards and upwards, past the Doric Temple, also designed by Henry Flitcroft (He did OK from the first Marquis!), and then on to Wentworth Woodhouse.

Another folly? This time it's a Doric Temple.

We thought the grounds of Wentworth Woodhouse would be open to the public but not so. Interestingly, it's the largest private residence in the UK and is also double fronted, although we didn't get to see the back front, only the front front.

The architecture is Palladian (we thought that was either a horse or element 46 – neither, we were wrong) and after 60 years of being closed the house is now being renovated and reopened judiciously.

Wentworth Woodhouse- quite magnificent.

The important bit at the front.
– couldn't get the mower to move though!

The grounds are broad and spreading and with a great feeling of openness. On leaving the estate we passed another fine building that had a sundial <u>and</u> a clock strapped to its bell tower, not seen that before - bell tower, clocks and sundials all in the same housing. Talk about belts and braces!

Sundials, clocks and bells in the same housing.

And at the main gate we turned left past the micro-brewery, what looks like old stables and an appalling pong reinforcing the idea of stables (wonder what the beer tastes like?) and into Wentworth.

Not right by the war memorial, but on a bit and then right, to walk down a long broad path lined with daffodils to the Church; glorious – we came at just the right time of year.

A broad avenue of waymarkers.
(OK we'll let it drop now).

Wentworth Church.

Once past the Church, our walk took us into Elsecar, along field edges, open spaces, a tastefully converted windmill and the occasional puzzled look.

And that puzzled look again.

We found we'd missed the train back to Sheffield by about ten minutes. Next one in an hour.

In the pub.

Time then for some culture in the local hostelry: excellent service, lovely people and good beer – so good we nearly missed the train again.

We had learned that despite some amazing scenery, impressive buildings and excellent views the whole thing can be brought down by inconsiderate (and evidently ignored) fly tipping along the verges of the roads – things improved once away from the main roads though.

Walk 12. Conisbrough to Elsecar.

September 11th – overcast but pleasant.

The Don and the Dearne; a pleasant, but longish, walk where we were all on good form, saw lots of birds and plants – no idea what they were; bunged-up canals, sculptures, bridge art, over-arched paths and the odd wide vista. All interspersed with politics, Brexit and bad jokes.

Usual start to the day; into Sheffield, coffee and a breakfast snack, Dave handed out today's meals and we boarded the train to Conisbrough. We are saving the Castle for a later cultural event (Ivanhoe and all that good stuff).

Exit Conisbrough station from the back entrance and over the Don onto the memorial to Cadeby Main Colliery, behind this is the former Earth Centre which sadly had to close because of a lack of visitors. It seems to be used today as a centre for pointless 'corporate bonding' – one of the more pointless activities dreamed up by pointless high-A management.

Tributes to a closed colliery.

And a placid river Don.

The path is easy to find, tarmac and a gentle up hill by the side of the former Earth Centre. As we walked past the closed gates there was a group of people in the centre of what looked like the parade ground, huddled in some kind of 'team-talk' (shudder).

The path by the side of the Earth Centre.

The path climbs gently up hill through some pleasant woods to skirt round the top of the Earth Centre with a wide and pleasant view over the countryside and a view of what looks like an army camp below:

Shouting & hollering – bonding!

Looking the other way – a lot better.

And now the walk starts proper – we've successfully navigated the station and found the right path for a shortish distance before we leave the river Don and walk over the river Dearne which is to be our companion for much of the journey, taking us over fields, through a nature reserve and across busy roads where the drivers aim for you as you try to cross.

Crossing the Dearne – we were to do this three times.

The Dearne, lots of flowers which didn't photograph too well.

Historically, the Dearne has been very heavily polluted as it flows from Denby Dale through Barnsley and Mexborough to join the Don some distance downstream. Thankfully, over the last thirty years or so the West Riding River Board has cleaned things up – as evidenced by the number of anglers we saw.

The Path.

We are now on the Trans Pennine Trail which we followed for the rest of the day.

The first of the Trans Pennine Trail signs.

From this point on there is little of real significance that demands description, so the next bit of the walk will be described by annotated photographs which show the path and also the various signs to look out for; interspersed with odd comments and the odd photo of a plant or something we considered interesting – which is a bit back-to-front because normally there are lots of words and a few photos.

The trail – wide vista, easy walking.

Walking the flood barrier along the Dearne.

A government admin repository?

Crossing the Dearne.

The Dearne from the bridge.

And a path.

Turn right along the river.

Not shown here, the railway bridge has helpful height clearance markings in both imperial and metric. Judging by the brickwork, it's a pity they forgot to include width.

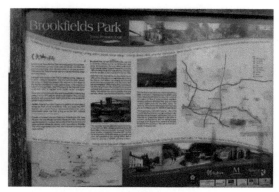
And into Brookfields Park.

Sculpture at the park entrance.

This piece of sculpture (that's the stone and metal bit) has lots going on – aquatic life, railways, homage to canals, falling rain and lots more.

The path continues quite uneventfully through Brookfields Park, with plants, wild life and the odd windfall of fruit – not sure why there are pear trees and crab apples dropping things over the path, perhaps we are passing through the remains of a grand house. And this took us to the place where we didn't get lost!

Having crossed the road, we came to the RSPB Old Moor bird sanctuary but the path appeared to be going back in a loop in the direction we had come from. The trees and bushes made it difficult to see very far, or what might lie to right and left.

Unlike each walk to date when we had reached a point where the path looked odd and we took what we thought was the way, we actually consulted the map and found we had to double back on ourselves for a short way. So we did.

Magic. The 'detour' was only a few yards and soon we were pointing in the right direction again with wetlands and a big pond that was the bird reserve. Only saw one person with binoculars though.

Despite two degrees in botany Steve is quite useless at plant identification (but then, as spurious justification, mathematicians can be quite poor at sums).

A blue flower.

Grumpy looking thing.

A yellow flower.

Pink flowers.

And some flowers in a bog.

The path again – with 'sculpted' handrail.

From here, the path continues under bridges and along rather small desolate drainage channels.

Mr Apollo **David holding up an undecorated bridge over a desolate drainage channel.**

And now a desolate bridge.

Over the next stretch there are several examples of *Bridge Art*.

Banksy, we miss you.

Some decorated bridges and their approaches.
(not in strict sequence)

At the end of the bird sanctuary are a couple of pieces of sculpture and immediately beyond there is a busy road to cross. Some motorists were OK but others seemed to be aiming for us; the only minor difficulty was that we couldn't tell which was which.

Sculpture at the end of the bird sanctuary.

More sculpture at the end of the bird sanctuary.
(Optional litter not included in the photo.)

And next, an insanely busy road.

Look out for this sign.

Not helpful is that the sign for the walk is hidden behind the vegetation that fills the central reservation.

And a path.

We are now following the Elsecar Branch Canal. A *Pennine Waterways* leaflet provides some lovely pictures of the canal higher up with people fishing and recreation all over the place. This end of the canal is a bit different though.

The canal is somewhere underneath the plank.

Further along, there has been volunteer restoration and a stretch of the canal has been recovered.

The recovered canal.

The Elsecar end of the canal terminates at a bridge where the arches are so small only a model boat would ever find its way through.

The other end of the canal with only enough space for very small boats to pass under the arches!

Another overarched footpath.

And on to Elsecar and the completion of this part of the journey; linking with the walk from Meadowhall.

A walk up the road towards the pub we used last time (the barmaid was good fun) past a long line of terraced cottages.

One occupant was perhaps a railway worker in days gone by; or perhaps an enthusiast. Elsecar boasts a heritage railway which we heard but didn't see (unlike Victorian children).

Once a railway worker?

A terraced row – of workers' cottages?

Elsecar Church and point where we meet the end of the walk from Meadowhall.

In the pub.

There are several welcoming hostelries in Elsecar so we called into one for a pint that was described by the brewer as *hinted with lavender, bergamot and cinnamon* (perhaps with just a gentle whiff of bullshit to round it out?)

We had learned that bridge art is creative and mostly well done, it certainly cheered us up; as did some of the sculpture – and, all for free.

On for a meal at another pub and a pint before catching the train back to Sheffield and home.

A very good day where we walked over 11 miles without aches and pains and felt we are getting fitter; good banter and old jokes.

Footnotes.

We enjoyed a wonderful example of unnecessary bureaucracy: at Elsecar station where you need to get a ticket from the machine in order to buy a ticket on the train or at Sheffield station; and after that, no ticket collector on the train and no barriers in Sheffield. Management?

And in the pub.

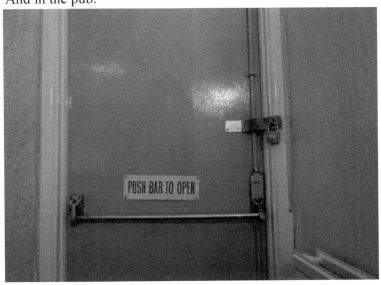

Health and safety alive and well?
Note the padlock.

Walk 13. Conisbrough to Doncaster.

February 21st 2019 – unseasonally warm and sunny.

A mix of contentment, reflection and peace following the majestic and slow-moving Don; mixed with unmitigated discontent, amazement and anger at the staggering incompetence of government and management – May, Brexit, self-interest and bugger-all concern for the people they were elected to represent. Anyway, enough of the soap-box and on with the walk.

Conisbrough station is easily reached by each of us, who arrived from different directions so there was a bit of time to kill waiting for the others. Lots of daydreaming and reflection (not much else to do, except perhaps train spotting?)

Conisbrough Station – a hive of inactivity.

Duly assembled we started with the now usual excellent bacon roll, a bit of catching-up and a look at the map to pick the route that will take us past the visitor centre and to the Don Valley Way and Trans-Pennine Trail.

Pit memorials made from reclaimed stainless steel.

Another look at the Cadeby and Denaby pit memorials. past the visitor centre, up to the gates by the former Earth Centre and on to the well-defined path, round the corner to the right and before long there is a fine view of Conisbrough castle, opened in 1190 and sufficiently majestic to inspire Sir Walter Scott to write Ivanhoe.

Conisbrough Castle, flag flying.

From here, the path is exceptionally well defined and follows the river so we failed to get lost and our only detour on this stretch of the walk was one we deliberately took – but more of that later.

The first major structure we happened upon was the Conisbrough viaduct, a splendid piece of civil engineering; the brickwork still looks good.

Conisbrough viaduct.

David, who understands bridges, explained that the thicker upright is introduced because if an arch collapses the whole thing could come down like a row of dominos. The thicker upright acts as a 'stopper'.

Following the Don we had plenty of time to reflect on the meaning of life, politics and days gone by; emerging before long by the *Sprotbrough Flash* Nature Reserve which was invaded by armies of twitchers with expensive cameras and significant lenses looking for a rare migrant. Sadly, we didn't catch sight of it and no-one saw fit to return a conversation – evidently focusing on the wildlife.

Then some more peaceful walking, but only as far as the Boat Inn; a delightful pub, looks good and with loads of character.

The Boat Inn.

A small beer in shirt-sleeves in the sunshine on the terrace (it's February you know!) and a reluctant leave to follow the mighty Don a bit further.

Benches by The Boat Inn.

This picture is included because Dave has a photo from 2007 of just the top rail of the middle bench projecting above floodwater – with three youths sitting on it.

The benches in 2007.

Flood management seems to have been improved a bit since then.

The path leads now to Engine Wood, so called because it is the site of the engine that used to pump water up to Sprotbrough Hall on the hill; you can only see a fence from down here and the Hall has been demolished, so not much of architectural interest; but, there is still the remains of the engine house and the pumping gear:

Pumping gear – a bit rusty now.

The walk continues along the easy path next to the Don with the A1 visible in the distance. From here, the traffic on the A1 gets progressively and insistently noisier.

The Don with the (noisy) A1 in the distance.

And this is February – we couldn't get over the warmth and the plants flowering all along the walk.

Don't these shrubs and things know what time of year it is?

It was just after Engine Wood that we made our deliberate detour, past Dave's old house to the Ivanhoe pub (throwback to Conisbrough Castle) for a light beer and a breather.

In the distance is the grade 1 listed Cusworth Hall, described by some as the jewel in Doncaster's crown; now a museum with an excellent rating and a big park to explore as well.

Cusworth Hall, looking across the A1.

Around here the continual white noise from the A1 is beginning to be very noticeable and our route will now lead us underneath it for the next part of the walk into Doncaster. Back on to the Trans Pennine Trail and – bridge art; we'd forgotten all about that, it's normally been by canal sides.

Bridge Art, censored for the more discerning reader.

Under the A1, along the river and yet another design of gate – one of the things we've noticed through the walk is the variety of interesting gates and also the number of gates that seem to serve no purpose whatsoever.

An interesting gate.

And on to the railway bridges where we stopped for a late lunch and then tried to decide which was the right way to Doncaster:

Do we go left or straight on?

The Trans Pennine Trail goes both left and straight on; we decided straight on, follow the river and then the Don Valley Way which is clearly marked with its own distinctive symbol.

The River Don.

Past a bloke sunbathing on the other bank (keep banging on about February) until we came to a point where the path forks; our route was over a bridge through barriers either end where some thoughtful person had removed a number of bars from the barriers to open the way to a well-trodden path by the prison.

Pretty close to Doncaster now, in sight of the prison and, the old railway works where the Flying Scotsman was built.

Doncaster prison.

The old locomotive works.

From here on in it would be rather difficult to get lost – prison wall on one side, river on the other; a bit further on the river is replaced with a green steel fence.

Out from the fence, past a couple of dodgy-looking characters (pleased there were three of us), up some steps to the road bridge with the Cathedral – St. George's Minster – over the road.

Quite hard to get lost on this leg of the journey.

Doncaster Cathedral.
(St. George's Minster)

Doncaster Street Art.
(our only cultural experience of the day)

In the (third) pub.

An excellent supper with good beer where we reflected on our learning experience that viaducts have a thicker pillar to prevent them falling over like a row of dominos if one of the spans fails – clever people those railway engineers.

Walk 14. Braithwaite to Doncaster.

July 2019 – weather back to normal.

A day in which we break David's heart by taking a taxi (very profligate), see a lady open a canal bridge, follow part of the Trans-Pennine-Trail, walk over more solid surface than before, work to the worst map yet and talk to a farmer.

Sunrise about 5:00 AM, easy to get up; just this side of chilly with high hazy clouds and a dab of sunscreen for the first time this year. We met in Doncaster at about 10:30, bacon sandwich, coffee, ring the taxi firm and off.

Coming out of Doncaster is like driving through Slough only more aromatic – turns out the taxi driver had a touch of flatulence. Once clear of the city, through some really pleasant country lanes. Detour round the Church in Barnby Dun to arrive at the car park by the New Junction Canal in Braithwaite.

This is the Braithwaite just north of Doncaster, not the one near Keswick; it sits west of Stainforth, not the one in the Dales which is west from Hatfield, not the Hertfordshire one that advertises the north. There's a good chance of getting lost before we start!

Disembark, pay the taxi, sort out provisions and don suitable headgear for the walk in a lovely warm July day, after a month of rain in the UK and the highest June temperatures recorded in Europe.

**Lovely day; Suitable headgear.
Very British.**

125

A passing note about Yorkshire dialect: Braithwaite arrives a bit early at the mill and the foreman says "morning Braithwaite, how are you?" Braithwaite replies "Who's *thee* to *you* me when ah'm *tha* to *thoo*?". Nominative, Accusative, Dative and Ablative in the same sentence (Latin scholars please note) – can't do that with *textspeak*.

Canal bridge by the car park.

A bit of a frustrating start because everything in your being suggests you should follow the canal towards Doncaster; but not so, we turn our backs on the canal and head down Braithwaite Lane to follow the Trans Pennine Trail which is well marked with blue signs and the number 62. The really clear markings are needed because this part of the Trail follows very few natural features or boundaries.

Following the road, which is a feature of this stretch, we pass a hut in a garden which doubles as a café and also a place where your Trans Pennine Trail's (TPT to the initiated ones) record sheet can be stamped with your Proof Of Original Passage Enthusiastically Recorded (POOPER) for the passing walkers to demonstrate they have completed certain sections on the Trail.

Hut, Café and Stamping Point.

We've had a few dry days recently and crops are being sprayed; with the sun behind the sprayers the small rainbows look quite attractive; should be quite easy to find their ends with a bit of triangulation and uncover the crock of gold. We still had eleven miles to cover, so didn't bother.

The route follows the road which has no footpaths – like many of the roads round here, so we adopted the Boy Scout approach and walked on the right-hand side of the road which was fine until a white van rounded a blind bend and missed us by inches.

Brains into gear (like the white van) as we changed from side to side of the road so we could see more clearly. Or, more importantly, the various motorists could see what was ahead of them (us!)

This is not a bus shelter.

By the side of the road we thought we saw a bus shelter – so there is civilisation (at least on a couple of days a week), but it turned out this is where the various parish notices are posted, and over the road is a bench which looks like the place where the parish meetings are held.

The sign on the back of the bench reads:
THORPE IN BALNE PARISH MEETING.
The council meets on sunny days presumably.

This is actually confusing because the parish notices come a long way before Thorpe in Balne; we still have to pass though Trumfleet before turning right to Thorpe in Balne.

Trumfleet marker.
Note the gap at the bottom;
something must have given it one hell of a thump.

And now, serious disappointment.

One of the things we have noticed on this walk is the amount of wayside litter – cans and bottles (no doubt thrown from cars) and fly tipping – everything from rolls of carpets to the pile photographed here:

A bloody disgrace – complete with shopping trolley.

A short way on is a clear signpost directing us to the right indicating Thorpe in Balne is only half a mile away.

A pair of red kites were circling in the thermals, looking quite lazy (which we're sure they're not), past sheep with new lambs (noisy little things), past some very smart properties and past yet more copies of the minutes etc. of the parish meetings.

The road seemed to just go on, and on, and on.

A spectacular front garden.

Are we nearly there yet?

Overtaken by a monstrous piece of agricultural machinery we stopped to watch the hay being turned into one long Mohican haircut; years ago it used to be tedded into four rows.

We got chatting to the farmer who explained that modern farming equipment was well automated and computer controlled.

The tractor will now circle the field, its computer will map it and then the most economical route will be automatically chosen (we thought one of those would be good for us today as we seemed to be walking in the wrong direction at every opportunity).

Other very clever attachments are cameras that can be fitted to regulate seeding, spraying and fertiliser application.

Further along another machine was baling a cut and dried crop, turning out circular bales about every 50 yards, a bit like a monstrous egg-laying machine.

Just as at the start, all our instincts here were to turn left and head directly to Doncaster, but not to be – frustrated again we had to keep straight on, along more hot tarmac towards Owston Grange. The row of pylons is the marker and then a small signpost with 62 written on it where we turn right.

We came off the tarmac onto a concreted footpath (not much softer on the feet) with lissom branches overhanging, gentle sunlight dappling the recalcitrant walkway with a cerulean sky overhead. The blossom appears almost luminous whilst effulgent insects zig-zag through the fulsome foliage to disturb the arcadian moment.

But enough of the Les Dawson and back to the walk.

Over the railway line (close the gates behind you), past some more agriculture which is more aromatic than earlier and in a short distance we're back onto tarmac (oh joy), walking over one railway bridge and under another to then arrive at the level crossing.

Over.

Under.

And across.
Thought they'd got rid of steam engines.

And on to another wide, hard surfaced track – with litter. This track divides and we turn left, actually pointing towards Doncaster for the first time today. Through a stile, into the shade and time for lunch.

Pied, tomatoed, trifled and chocolated we followed the Trail where the parachuted seeds littered the track like snow (Les Dawson thankfully skipped for this bit).

Almost like snow.

Like a big snowflake.

Follow the Trail and the signs, over the railway – again, along more road – again, past hay being baled – again, across a stream and on to a track. Easy on the feet.

An actual track.

But, before you know it, we're onto hard surface again to walk past Bentley Park which is a significant open space with courts, skateboard park, kiddies play areas and all-in-all an excellent local amenity.

The Trail turns right, opposite the main gates – one of the few turns that is not that well marked. Through some houses and follow the trail. The path widens and enters trees for about half a mile where there is a junction and a cycling group mending a puncture.

At this junction the Trans Pennine Trail goes straight ahead, our trail bears left to follow the ***Doncaster Link Route*** to the city centre. Blue sheds behind a wall on the left act as markers.

It was a short way down the Link Route that we found an unusual bench – dedicated to *The Stirling Single*; a railway engine with just one driving wheel that's eight feet diameter and to demonstrate the fact there's a model of the engine underneath – most peculiar.

An unusual bench. (Note the model train underneath).

The seat is high enough off the ground for us to sit with feet dangling, like youngsters learning their times tables.

Before long we met the railings that seem to typify Doncaster and emerge onto a main road. Turning right across the level crossing we kept straight on; the signage isn't that great and we nearly continued round the corner.

After so much road, this bit seemed to go on for ever, past community centres and several places where you can't play on the grass; eventually we came to a bridge where the path turns left along the disused railway and into Doncaster proper.

Over the Don.

Crossing a bridge over the river Don we headed for St. George's Church which is a prominent landmark and in a direct line to Wetherspoons.

<u>In the pub.</u>

Wetherspoons. It was curry night – so we had fish and chips – washed down with rehydrating and very refreshing lager. Really good and most welcome.

An excellent day where we learned that those dedicated walkers who officially complete the Trans-Pennine-Trail with a fully stamped record card can officially show off their POOPER.

Walk 15. Braithwaite to Snaith.

January 2020 – between two weather systems.

Taxi to Braithwaite, where we had started the earlier walk to Doncaster so we could now walk in the opposite direction following the Trans Pennine Trail. One of the longer walks but alongside a still, calm canal followed by significant mud. A bit concerned about timing with only eight or so hours of daylight, made it reasonably comfortably though.

Arrived Doncaster about 10:00 AM, coffee, bacon sandwich, called a mini-cab which is a lot cheaper than the station taxi-rank to start at the car park by the New Junction Canal in Braithwaite.

From the lift-bridge looking north.

A beautiful day, peaceful and warm for January with a long flat walk along the canal beckoning.

Another lift-bridge over a very calm canal.

After a couple of cyclists rode by – one with a duck-call instead of a bell; different and effective. We were on our own except for a horse that kept us company for a little distance but by walking single file whilst it examined some grass, we managed to overtake it and leave it behind.

Our companion for some of the way.

The path crosses the canal at Sykehouse lock which is well signed and impossible to miss; there is a swing-bridge here with a mechanism like a roller-coaster, one set of wheels run along the top and a second set of wheels sit underneath the flange (if that's the right term) to keep the thing level.

Swing-bridge mechanism – like that of a roller-coaster.

Before crossing the bridge, there's a prophetic sign post to Fishlake a village that suffered terribly in the 2019 floods, was cut off for days and largely ignored by the 'great and good' in Westminster. Still recovering some months later. Mud to follow.

Prophetic sign-post to Fishlake.

Now on the other side of the canal.

A badly photographed gnome.

About a mile further along there is Sykehouse Road bridge; over the bridge and into the village, which has its fair share of idiosyncrasies, starting with an anti-aircraft gun in a front garden.

Sykehouse should be safe from air attack.

Then past the Primitive Methodist Chapel (working people's less regulated place of worship – nicknamed the Prims).

Never seen a primitive chapel before.

And a significant narrow-gauge railway in an equally significant garden.

And a railway enthusiast.

Past the model railway into Starkbridge Lane which is a bit overhung – and bloody midges; at this time of year!

And still not dry – another portent.

Following the excellent signage, the path goes through Topham, across the river Went and alongside fields of deep mud (remember Fishlake).

It could be easy to take a wrong turning over the next mile or so and the map came out a couple of times because the Trans Pennine Trail follows field edges, lots of right angles and a couple of wrong paths that look quite inviting.

This part of the walk is a significant detour because about a mile of the New Junction Canal – the one we have been following so far – appears to be private and with no way over to the other side of our next canal, Knottingly & Goole (part of Aire & Calder Navigation), so a detour of something like four miles.

Knottingly & Goole Canal – with boats!

After the four mile detour the path crosses the canal at Crow Croft Bridge to bear right and through the remains of a railway bridge with the track and arch removed. Through the bridge the various power stations come into view: Ferrybridge, Eggborough, Drax.

The lovely Yorkshire countryside.

Now the prophecies: Fishlake and the sodden fields, into more flat land. Great big meadows that stretch into the distance, very open and no doubt lovely in summer. All is peaceful here, except the sound of clay pigeon shooting and the M62 in the distance.

And now the mud.

After about a mile of mud the Trail bears left and then turns right along a hedge; a very wet track leads to a farm which must have some quite big children, judging by the size of the Lego bricks.

A little Dave relaxes with his Lego.

A dryish track heads off to the left and looks like it is going under the motorway. Ignore this and keep going for longer than seems necessary.

The fields are littered with what looks like landfill; we speculated this was as a result of the recent excessive wind and rain.

Further on to a minor road and a scout camp, past a road maintenance depot and over the M62.

And over the M62.

The Trail follows the road into West Cowick, to a T-Junction, where bus times to Selby are displayed and decisions made as to how many beers to enjoy whilst waiting for the next bus.

Turning left the road runs into Snaith; our timing has been good, after quite a few miles we arrive in daylight as the last of the schoolchildren make their way (singly) home. Into Snaith, down the hill to a roundabout, turn right and the start of the next leg is a little way ahead past the half-timbered building.

Snaith; the half-timbered building and start-point for the next leg.

But, how do they get buses on <u>both</u> sides of the road?

<u>In the pub.</u>

With a bit of time to kill before the bus we knocked most of the mud off our boots and enjoyed a pint to round off the day. We learned about the power of mud, something we would pick up again when walking from Bielby to Holme-on-Spalding-Moor.

We left for the bus with time to spare. It was late, but chatting to a couple of patient locals kept our spirits up and we were eventually off to Selby and home.

Interlude.

A picture from when it was dry.

Real Yorkshiremen.

Walk 16. Snaith to Selby.

Mid-March 2020, after three months of rain.

A day in which we saw the aftermath of some of the worst flooding ever suffered in the UK, found May blossom in March, marvelled at the clouds of midges so early in the year, nice and level – a flood plain.

Transport in the area has been disrupted by the weather and several road bridges were closed; we decided that two cars was the right approach. Normally we would have caught the train to Selby and the bus to Snaith in order to walk back and enjoy a couple of beers – but not to be.

Because of the weather, the road journey involved a number of detours and took quite a long time; finally, parking up we set off across the railway towards Selby.

This company used to sell sheds.

And this firm once sold classic cars.

Ten days after the flood the mess was clear to see, even though things had improved considerably with colossal pumps working day and night to empty the fields through 12" (30 cm) pipes.

Just a few of the big pipes.

The area had drained sufficiently for us to walk along the flood barrier which was accessed by turning back on ourselves from the left-hand pathway and heading down to the flooded fields.

The path is at the bottom right-hand corner. The river Aire is visible in the distance as a thin ribbon of water behind the flood.

This walk is exceptionally well marked with big blue signs – which is a good thing because later there is quite a bit of walking around field edges where it felt like we were doubling back all the time. We weren't.

Big blue signs.

The flooding has done quite a good job of clearing out some of the fly tipping and riverside debris, leaving a tide-mark along the bank that is the first part of the walk.

Tide-mark stretching into the distance.
The walk is along the top of this flood barrier.

At the end of the flood barrier the path opens into the road to Temple Hirst; this is the start of the daffodils which were out and almost shouting at us for the rest of the day.

Daffodils brightening up the roadside.

Magnolia, Gorse, May and errrr… something else.
Spring is definitely in the air – whatever the weather!

A bit of autumn colour to still enjoy.

And a reminder of how wet it has been recently.

The Aire takes a fairly sharp bend at Temple Hirst and here we take a right turn away from the river and over fields.

The bend in the river Aire – still a bit full.

A significant amount of debris had been deposited on the bank of the bend, testament to the volume of water that must have flowed past here a couple of weeks ago.

Quite a lot of debris.

The next mile or so is uneventful, following the road and making use of the blue signs where it feels like we were retracing our steps. It was along this bit when we eventually realised that the Drax power station is visible from just about everywhere.

Cross the railway and after what seems like even more doubling back come to Burn Airfield – the one used by Bomber Command during the war and still quite impressive with acres of tarmac, a bit overgrown now. It could make a decent alternative to expanding Heathrow!

A bit of runway.
- with the inevitable Drax in the background.

The path follows the railway line which runs alongside the edge of the airport and, contrarily, this was the only part of the walk where the flooding was deep enough to come over the standard hiking boot – slosh, slosh, slosh, bugger – a bootful.

This is the path.

Out on to the road, right then left by the level crossing and back alongside the railway as far as the Selby Canal which was to be our companion for the rest of the walk.

Despite fishing points at regular short intervals, it seemed strange that the canal was deserted, perhaps still repairing homes after the weather.

Selby canal looking quite moody.

Into Selby, a minor road leads to an industrial estate, ignore this and take the main road which is above us on a bridge. Up to the bridge, follow round and there's the car below in the station car park.

After so much walking on roads it was good to get out of boots and into soft shoes to return to Snaith where we arrived mid-late afternoon with everything closed. The cultural interlude was to visit the Church which we found was the first refuge in times of emergency with some lovely people feeding the Emergency Services, camp beds drying in the transepts and rations laid out to be taken as necessary. Coffee and a contribution, then time for tea. Nothing open in Snaith, so away up the road to Carlton.

In the pub.

A couple of miles on is the Odddfellows Arms (note the spelling); lovely people, good food and lots of it. Recommended.

We had learned about the power of flooding and the damage water can inflict on so many people; probably be a very long time before things get back to normal around here.

Replete, but thoughtful, we headed home.

Section 3: SELBY TO MALTON

I take over from here and after formative years in the West Riding, left for Liverpool in the mid-late 1960 when The Beatles ruled and the city was the centre of the known universe; one privilege was to visit the original Cavern the first time it had a licensed bar (it was quite disagreeable – even for a 19-year old).

Having qualified as a biologist with some original work into heavy metal tolerance (during flower-power!) there was little demand for an environmentalist in those days; we just kept pouring fumes from lead tetraethyl into the atmosphere and poisoning the Black Forest, so I joined the food industry on the basis that biology is how plants and animals are put together and food technology is how to take them apart again.

I had some good successes as I moved from product development to market development to business development and finally was smug enough to leave the multinationals and became a self-employed business consultant where I supported a good number of companies to grow, improve profitability and develop in a rapidly changing commercial world.

After retiring I moved back to Yorkshire, marked exam papers for a bit of income, wrote a couple of books and got back in touch with Dave and David when we decided to create a walk that joined our homes. We had much to catch up on – and still have – which we shared as we walked and hopefully captured some of our enjoyment in this book.

Steve.

And Selby Abbey.

Where we reject a truly miserable taxi firm, David lost and found his wallet; the fresh, bracing wind from hurricane Irma was in our faces most of the way. We learned about wind breaks, studies of clouds and saw lots of cows and calves – mostly on our path! We calculated the width of a UK standard cow, recognised why there are so many swing bridges on the Ouse and ended with a welcome cup of tea, a chat and some culture in Selby Abbey.

Earlier Dave and Steve had done a two-car exercise from Selby to Wressle because David had had to manage some client work. This time it was Dave's turn to look after a client so David and Steve decided to do the same journey but backwards.

Both walks are amalgamated in the interests of brevity; the earlier walk had been undertaken before we decided to have a "Cultural bit" so this had to be added and we visited Selby Abbey.

En-route we had discovered that taxis aren't that expensive (unless you leave your wallet in one!) when divided amongst the three of us (or even two this time), so instead of the two-car procedure we took a train to Selby and then a taxi to Wressle.

It is widely known that there are taxis readily available at *most* UK stations, ready and waiting to take you *anywhere* you ask. But *not at* Selby! At 9.15am we were casually told that the next cab from Station Taxis would be in three hours!

After checking that there were no trains to Wressle at a reasonable time and there were no buses in the turning circle masquerading as a bus station, we decided to visit the town centre past the abbey and look for another taxi!

We did find an *old* yellow upright type, not far from the Abbey – was this a cast off from Derby? Anyway, it worked so we took it.

Arrived in Wressle, seemed quite a long journey – and we were going to walk all the way back. David insisted on paying some of the taxi fare, good job he offered because he discovered his wallet missing – panic!

Lots of pocket patting, no luck; perhaps down the side of a seat, the driver was patient, good humoured and smiling gently (nice chap). Wallet found, sigh of relief, pulse rate dropping. It was down the back seat of the aged taxi. Walk started.

By the side of the Church (dedicated to St. John of Beverley) down to the Derwent, chatted to a local man walking his dog, commented on the wind; out now from the shelter of the trees and on to the top of the flood bank – this was to be our path for the next ten miles or so.

Then we noticed the wind – a bloody gale, but thankfully quite balmy, still hard work walking against it though. This was to be a recurrent theme of the day.

The start – along the flood bank.

The river was nicely full, but then it had been raining heavily on the North York Moors and the next things we noticed were the cows standing belligerently (of course) in the middle of <u>our</u> path; we contrived to walk confidently but gently towards them, they recognised our superiority and reluctantly made way for us – another recurring theme.

We arrived at Loftsome road bridge on the A63 where the map showed paths either side of the Derwent. The earlier walk (Dave & Steve) had been up the north bank and unsure about walking across the flood barrier about three miles further on, we elected to keep to the north side.

So up to the road bridge, life in your own hands, cross over and change river banks.

And down the north side of the river.

A slightly overgrown green sign clearly designated this as a public footpath but the funny gate had been broken, fenced over and barbed wired (no doubt to keep ramblers out, and cows in); but we are Queen's Scouts so climbed over with a bit of huffing and puffing – determined to do our bit to keep this footpath open.

Wind – bloody wind.

Full river, interesting eddy currents presumably caused by lots of water and the wind blowing generally upstream – even the river is fighting against it.

Cows – more bloody cows, this lot looked like heifers (Think it's spelled right) didn't want to get too close; confident but gentle walk, superiority established, uneventful passage.

At this time, we noticed two tracks along the top of the flood barrier – about the same width as a tractor's tyres but it seemed a strange place to drive a tractor on a regular basis.

Upon closer examination, the footprints indicated these were parallel cow tracks, walking two by two to who knows where; later we noticed three tracks that narrowed to two. You can tell from this how little we were looking around taking things in – too busy, head down, fighting the wind.

Over the river is the Drax Power Station – a big and impressive set of buildings, we were to walk round three sides of this thing as we followed the meanderings of the river. David reckoned we would see an ox-bow lake if we were to hang around for another 50,000 years or so.

Drax Power Station.

Drax is one of the biggest solid fuel fired Power Stations in the UK. It has since been modified (to reduce carbon emissions) by burning "Biomass" a fuel that is developed from organic materials, allegedly a renewable and sustainable source of energy used to create electricity or other forms of power. Should be carbon neutral, but is that counting the transport half way round the world, or not....?

Then occasional periods of calm coincided with clumps of trees that must have been acting as windbreaks, something we hadn't considered since our geography lessons fifty-odd years ago.

Neither had we recognised how efficient trees are at breaking the wind – but then look at America's Dust Bowl where trees and hedges were removed in the interests of efficiency.

More cows – this lot with calves, very wary, big eyes watching our every move so we were a bit circumspect, especially as the one at the far end of the herd had some quite magnificent horns!

Decided we would divert from this section of path to give the mothers and their babies some space. Further on, a farmer had posted a helpful notice that cows with calves can get a bit tetchy, which is OK – if you happen to be travelling the other way.

Hunger setting in but where to stop – bloody wind made sitting to eat all but impossible, but at last – the flood barrier (and yes, you can get across it) with a high wooden fence and a bench to 'sit and gaze' dedicated to a kind soul who must have enjoyed sitting here watching the boats (none today – too bloody windy).

First packed meal, very welcome and a very welcome sit-down; pushing against the incessant wind had felt like permanent uphill.

From downstream Derwent to upstream Ouse, dip down behind the flood barrier for a short way and then back up the flood barrier, interesting meanders, broad curves in the river, beacons on the bends, the odd sheep and the odd respite as trees broke the wind which must be pretty regular, if the lean on the trees was anything to go by.

Trees bowed over by persistent wind.

There was an interesting low level willow that gave the impression of a huge swan's nest!

Not much to report for the next couple of miles other than pleasant landscape, and Hemingbrough, whose Church can be seen for quite a long way and which we seemed to have encircled at least twice (and where we could have cut off a corner – but that would have been cheating!)

Hemingborough Church – quite distinctive.

Passed an area where the flood waters obviously cut into the bank and had created a large area just like a beach but unfortunately of mud! No sun-bathing there then.

Still the full river, cows and wind. Hunger beginning to set in again but where to stop? Had a lie-down by a fishing lake but difficult to eat horizontally so gave that up after a short rest and a wet bum. Interesting clouds scudding by and clouds at different heights moving in opposite directions!

And now! A barn – protected by barbed wire but acting as a brilliant wind-break (about five yards of peace) so settled on David's free (reject) cycle cape and enjoyed pulled pork with stuffing in ciabatta bread before lying back and cloud watching again.

Looking at the clouds, it was fascinating how fast the lower layer was moving – the higher altocumulus clouds were quite static; must have been reasonably pleasant seven miles up.

The shapes of the clouds were quite intriguing and it's easy to see where the ancients found their mythical beasts.

Clean-cut sheep.

Press on, feeling refreshed and rested, rounded the corner of the barn – back into the bloody gale. Fields still to be harvested even at this late stage, Drax looking a bit forbidding, some clean-cut sheep and yet more cows.

David thought these sheep looked as if they had had an Afro haircut but that may have had racist undertones so we decided it wasn't. However, he did try to identify the type of sheep. later, from the 74 British breeds.

This proved a big challenge with the close wool and pink clean cut faces. The conclusion was that they were either Border Leicester or Scotch Halfbred? Something to watch for again and ask a farmer.

**Steve doing the little boy (Compo?) walk on the wall.
Pretending it's windy – it was.**

The first of three swing bridges was the next interesting feature; in all there are three swing bridges around Selby, the rail bridge engineered to tolerances of less than a millimetre (the thickness of a pencil line); don't normally think of precision engineering with a thousand or so tons of steel.

Two of the swing bridges.

There are a number of major swing bridges downstream of the flood barrier to upstream of Selby, these include: Goole (railway), Boothferry (road), Selby by-pass (a modern bridge), Selby rail bridge and Selby road bridge. Upstream there is another swing bridge over the road in the village of Cawood. This is probably as many as the rest of the country put together?

We mused on the number of swing bridges in such a small area of UK geography. David, who understands bridges, pointed out that there had been these bridges in the days of sail to allow masted ships to come by, and once the right of way has been established, it must be maintained unless conceded.

Our conclusion is that the bridges were in place to allow galleons to sail into York (not much call for that today though). We wondered if the Vikings actually come to York that way and concluded 'probably not' as us Brits would surely have left the bridges closed just to annoy them.

And a third swing bridge.

The culture bit for today was to be Selby Abbey, founded before the Norman conquest, and lots of history. So, we headed into Selby, over the road bridge and on to the Abbey for a cup of Yorkshire tea and a bit of culture before a well-earned pint.

Selby's Coat of Arms.

159

Selby Abbey.

Dog tooth arches, lady behind a desk asking for Gift Aid donations; we donated in the café gift shop instead. Cup of tea really welcome after being dehydrated in the continuous bloody wind. The abbey has much to appreciate and enjoy.

Selby is the origin of the stars and stripes – the Washington coat of arms (three stars and three stripes) that got commandeered and aggrandised by George and turned into a flag.

The original Stars & Stripes.

It's in one of the higher abbey windows and quite hard to spot, so probably not important enough in those days to command a lower eye-level setting.

The second best Jesse window in England after York Minster.

And a funny old instrument (a serpent).

There are lasting mementos to the Mineworkers' Union from each of the pits in the Selby Coalfield.

A super coalfield to beat all others, massive thick seams of coal and enough to last a very long time – the coal seams had large faults which made them less economical and possibly the realisation of Carbon emissions and Miners v. Maggie strikes mean the pits are no more.

So, interestingly, instead of regimental flags hanging over the aisle as in most large places of worship there are the colliery banners.

Each banner has been carried proudly at the various marches and rallies. The NUM website is well worth a visit and Selby Abbey features in their struggle (still) for justice and reparation.

Two of the miners' banners.

We will not forget or forgive.

<u>In the pub.</u>

And now, after all this culture (and wind); it's time for a pint (or several) in the George – great ambience, enjoyable beer, extremely competent barmaid and genuinely good food at a reasonable price.

Over dinner, we calculated that the width of a standard UK cow would be of the order of 1½ metres, judging by the separation between the tracks they make walking side by side.

We also learned that America's Stars & Stripes originated in Selby and wondered how Her Majesty would feel if the Union Jack had originated in Paris.

During all this pondering we considered the next bit of the walk which seemed a bit far but, because much of it is on old railway track, we decided we were fit enough.

Then, to the station, and home (subject to trains possibly running late due to hurricane Irma laying trees on the line).

Walk 18. Holme-on-S. Moor to Wressle.

Or: Are we nearly there yet?

In which we realised that Wressle is the end of public transport as we know it; an earlier sortie identified a bus that ran twice a week (full of sheep and chickens with people turning out to wave) and an express from York that didn't stop anywhere. Some trepidation today because in the Middle Ages we would be entering the bit on the map which reads: **Here be Dragons.** *We also missed a turning (as usual) twice.*

This time we used the two-car technique, meeting in Wressle then travelling to Holme-on-Spalding Moor for breakfast – a cup of coffee and a bacon sandwich – to start our walk along the Bubwith Rail Trail – another of those country walks kindly donated by the good Dr. Richard Beeching around 1963 – easy to find and picturesquely hemmed in by lines of trees most of the way.

A little way down the trail.

The result of being hemmed in though means there's not much to look at except the local vegetation and the odd cultivated field.

So, it's unexciting. But thankfully we had brilliant sunshine (plenty of sunblock) and, as always, our own good company with lots currently happening in a world that needed to be put to rights – which we did.

We parked in Spen Lane – interesting because that's the name of one of the streets near West Riding's Birkenshaw where we grew up; but looks nothing like the one in the old days.

We set off along the rail trail full of bacon and coffee; Dave kindly lent Steve a hat as protection from the sun (no pictures because he looked a complete prat). David turned into a legionnaire for the day (and, to be fair) he looked a bit daft too.

By accident, we were walking west so the sun was to the side and behind – a good thing because it was quite bright.

Wait…For It.   **You 'Orrible Little man.**   **H'atten-Shun.**
Legionnaire David.

It struck us that this must be awful on a drizzly day, so we had picked well, after three weeks of drought and one of the warmest weeks this year.

The bright sun and overarching green went on for a bit and then through a break in the bushes, trees and shrubs was a ploughed field which looked purple – strange soil, this. After some discussion Dave reckoned it was the eye seeing the complementary colour – a bit like in those optical illusion books.

Past a dead vole, rabbits, left-behinds from foxes and lots of insects. Buzz, flap sting, pierce – one of the little buggers even drew blood.

After a couple of miles, the track suddenly stops and decamps us by the roadside; we followed the road, ignoring the layby opposite and the possibility of the track continuing on the other side of the road (despite being clearly marked on the map) but it was a while since we had checked the route and of course Steve had researched it thoroughly beforehand.

Walking past the country park (lodges for sale, very good prices) we had that twinge of self-doubt, that comes from long experience, and got out the map (unusual for blokes to seek directions) to find the trail had indeed crossed the road; usefully there is a track to meet it a hundred yards or so past some jumbled tractor tyres and bits of machinery.

Excitement over.

Back on track.

Back on the rail trail and not far ahead what looked like one of the rows of trees that grow along river banks; we must be close to the Derwent and the descent into Wressle. No such luck, a small stream that was little more than nuisance value.

On and on and on, broken by three people coming in the opposite direction: ey-up, na-then, sithee, 'ow do, helleough.

And on and on and on and on, another row of trees, another small stream – this time with fish to watch; are we nearly there yet? No.

And on...

And on and on and on and on and on, the wonderful solitude broken only by a chap with a lovely little black (and wet, and smelly) dog; who described a circular route that went under the M62 – fascinating.

On the way we had passed a number of overgrown station platforms – or what had once been platforms and according to the old OS Sheet 98 these were the stations for: Holme on Spalding Moor, Foggathorpe, Highfield and Bubwith with, what looked like, a goods depot at Allberries – four stations in seven miles. OK when no-one drove, but today vindicates Beeching to some extent.

Reminded us of Flanders & Swann's song *The Slow Train* – it's on YouTube.

Across a road (Wressle to Bubwith) and could not help noticing the posh houses that stretched away in either direction.

We also began to notice the ground sloping away on either side of the path which signals the approach to a bridge – over a significant river, not a piddling stream.

And on and on and on and on and on and on, another row of trees, are we nearly there yet – yes we are !!!!!

It's about lunch time and dropping down to river level we looked ahead at open fields and a flood barrier with the Breighton Ferry pub in the distance – open ground, early afternoon and blazing sun.

Even though the bridge had been dismantled there were still the flood arches – shade for lunch and somewhere to rest for a while – on hardened mud (Steve's trousers were something to behold – skidmarks on the *outside*).

Enjoyed a sausage butty, cheesecake, Bakewell tart (insert old jokes here).

And a banana.

And flies.

And another dollop of sunscreen.

The flood arch – shade, lunch, mud and flies.

We then followed the flood barrier past a pump which was irrigating the fields (harvest in, large round bales lying around – so hard to see why).

Past some quite alarmingly large cows, a few with calves; us taking strategic detours, as appropriate, in order to avoid two tons of grumpy beef spoiling the day.

A day being occasionally interrupted by a biplane doing (vomit-inducing) aerobatics and some smaller fixed-wing planes and an RAF jet too high to see.

And so, to the Breighton Ferry; a pub we had hoped would be open at lunchtime for a shandy or glass of lemonade – no such luck.

Back in March, Steve had checked out (most of) the route including the public footpath across the field away from the pub into Breighton village. It was then deep in mud and impassable – almost ruined a pair of sturdy shoes.

However, after three weeks of unbroken drought and sunshine it now looked to be worth a try; evidently not a popular path judging by the lack of 'boot erosion' and, at the Breighton end, still muddy despite the recent sun and drought.

**Last week, this was a not very popular path.
Now thoughtfully flattened for us by the landowner.**

Into Breighton village; quite a longish walk, unbroken other than by the yapping of a small dog protecting a posh house; it all seemed a bit too far so we got the map out (again) and asked the question 'are we nearly there yet?' – no we aren't, keep going to where the road proper runs out; by a posher house.

This is where we turned right and away from the friendly village of Breighton (after the second friendly sign).

A friendly(?) sign – sort of modern Rosetta Stone?

We now walked along a significant track across fields, between a range of crops – barley, rape, potatoes – where the dry weather was quite evident.

Compare this with the not-so-popular path.

Wressle castle was just visible in the distance; spirits raised, we were getting close.

And then. The path just stopped by a stream with high hedges, brambles, mud and general unwelcomeness.

Whilst we studied the map (again) David went for a wander and decided to turn left, the map is wrong (yes – it <u>is</u> wrong) and so was the old OS Sheet 98; the path did a left and a right, not a straight on.

Back on track between crops getting ready to be harvested; hope there's no downpour (not unusual) to spoil the harvest after all this useful sunshine; and now on to the road and left into Wressle, past the castle and on to the car.

Wressle Castle.

Sit down in the car – boots off, bliss, then back to Holme-on-Spalding Moor for the second car.

<u>In the pub.</u>

A bit of a bind that we were driving, so minimal alcohol: small beer, lemonade and shandy, set the next three dates and reminisce about yomping 72 miles in a day and other significant (but now unattainable) challenges.

We were still remarkably supple after all these miles and learned that old railway lines make walking as easy as canals – the challenge is to make them interesting.

We turned our attention to the next bit which looks like quite a long way; this turns out not to be because the route sits across two maps and it's actually quite hard to follow the various tracks and paths that seem to come at you from all angles. We should have it sorted in time though.

It was too early for tea and with two of us driving we decided on an early finish, home and relax.

Walk 19. Bielby to Holme-on-S. Moor.

February 2020 – remarkably wet and windy. As a contrast, this time last year we were walking into Doncaster in sunshine and 19°C with a gentleman sunbathing on the other side of the river Don.

One of the few two-car parts of the trip, lots of mud and quite flat (hence the mud); we pondered on the weight of water to create this much mud, not much to report with the peace & quiet, the banter and the fresh (bracing) air a bit difficult to put into print. We concluded with three cultural visits.

A two-car walk; we met at Holme-on-Spalding Moor which had been the start point for the walk to Bubwith & Wressle, left one car there, had breakfast (the usual bacon sandwich) and drove to Bielby which is the start-point for the walk to Pocklington. We parked by the water-mill where there is a small car park and walked back into the village to have a look around before setting off by the side of St. Giles' Church.

Every house has a name, so no real need for street numbers. The local pub, The College Arms, is now closed, and apparently has been for some time – so forget this as a stop for dinner later.

We strolled to the bus stop with no buses, which seems to be the norm now in the Yorkshire countryside, past a house selling free-range eggs which we thought a bit odd as it's the chickens that are free range. Very soon the village turns into fields so we turned back on ourselves and walked to St. Giles' Church, and mud.

On the wall of the old Wesleyan Chapel. A home now for sale.
*Boast not thyself of to morrow for on thine
eyelids is the shadow of death.*
A cheerful lot the Victorians.

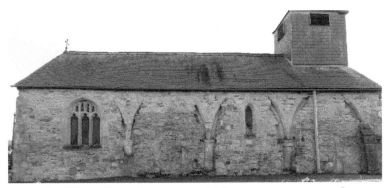

**St Giles Church – external plaster now removed
and sandstone walls restored. Locked, so no inside pics.**

Down the good road by the side of St. Giles to the *public footpath* signpost and the path across the field. This set the scene for much of the day.

This is the footpath!

Just by the copse at the other side of the field there is a foot bridge and a left turn down the side of the field along a beck; after half a mile or so the track emerges on to the road. We turned left and just past the road sign to Bielby turned right down a broad track that leads past some houses and to a T-junction in the track; we turned right along another good track which went by sodden fields, grouse feeders, and germinating crops.

The seedlings were doing their best and we pondered on the benefits of perhaps replacing wheat with rice.

**Crops now
beginning to sprout.**

**Carrots under here somewhere
– now ruined.**

With a zig and a zag we were approaching Seaton Ross and the end of relative dryness; into water-logged carrot fields and more mud. The path enters the town through an estate on to the main road opposite a house called Lonicera (Honeysuckle to you and me).

A left turn, through the town as far as the pub and then left again down a signposted track with a note to the effect that the local ramblers had been involved in its upkeep. Sadly, their efforts could not overcome the impact of the wind and rain we had 'enjoyed' over the last few weeks.

The track (mud) and a tree blown over in the recent gales.

The mud is relentless, occasionally giving way to ankle-deep water where, at a point on the map marked as *Lady Well* Steve got his boots filled; and spent the next twenty minutes or so splishing and sploshing (with a few grumbles!) until the water in his boots warmed up and socks absorbed what was left. The clue was in the name (Lady Well)!

Quite a significant tree – strong wind.

A few trails come together here.

Despite the trails becoming a bit confusing, we could see the blue square factory building on the road where we had parked earlier, so taking the right-hand mud track would lead to the finish about a mile away.

Take the right-hand fork.
Note what looks like elephant grass on the left.

The crops here were a bit different from those we had seen elsewhere with elephant grass possibly to feed Drax and carrots (to feed the horses?)

The elephant grass – for Drax?

Carrots exposed by the rain.
Sadly, rotted by the persistent wet.

The track continues past the boundary of a large house with paddocks, horses and a yapping dog, to the gate that is the start of the Bubwith Rail Trail.

The walk turned out to be a bit shorter than we had feared, albeit a bit damper than we had hoped. As it was early afternoon, we decided to spend the remainder of daylight absorbing some culture.

Three short cultural excursions

Excursion 1.
The Church of Holme-on-Spalding Moor.

Heading East on the A163 is a big square Church high up on a hill, with the usual helpful brown road sign pointing to it. A sharpish right turn off the main road, over the cattle grid (so you don't go up the hill sideways?) to the Church with ample parking.

The view is absolutely stunning; but it would appear that people aren't as keen to climb big hills today as they used to be:

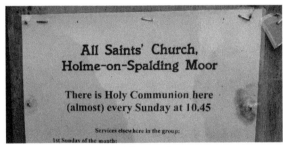

All Saints' Church, Holme-on-Spalding Moor

There is Holy Communion here (almost) every Sunday at 10.45

Services elsewhere in the group:
1st Sunday of the month:

Almost!

There's a proper old lychgate with a smaller gate to the side so the mourners can get past without having to climb over the pall bearers or the coffin, and a graveyard that has to be in one of the best settings in the county.

Inscription: "Till the morning break and the shadows flee away".

Holme-on-Spalding Moor graveyard.

<u>Excursion 2.</u>
The Church at Everingham.

Fields of Snowdrops behind the Church.

And Buttercups. – well Aconites actually.

Those buttercups, Steve, are aconites (aconites, winter; buttercups summer; remember?)

Driving back into Bielby to pick up the second car, we passed a large acreage of pig pens, the animals running around happily and, on the other side of the road, a very large aviary where grouse and pheasant are lovingly reared.

Seems a pity they'll all be shot in a couple of months.

By now it was getting a bit late and the need of a meal was getting more urgent; Steve changed out of his wet (but warm) boots and we headed for Market Weighton.

Excursion 3.
Market Weighton and Church No.3.

A very pleasant couple of hours. First, we visited the Church which has a 'Charities Board'; on the wall, something we have not seen anywhere before, some quite fine stained glass, then a couple of famous people and, finally, pie.

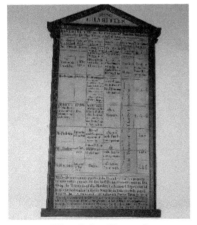

Charities Board.

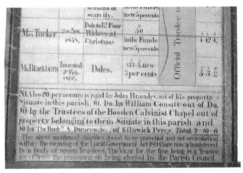

Bottom bit expanded and
sharpened up.

Detail from one of the windows.

**Yorkshire playing a part in South America
gaining independence from the Spanish.
First Venezuela and after that for all of South America.**

William Bradley.
England's tallest man at 7'9", or 2m 36cm.

And an interesting pub sign.

In the pub.

Churches, sightseeing and famous people over, time for dinner at the Griffin Inn. Excellent pie; pity we were driving, so the beer will have to wait for another time.

We learned that William Bradley was England's tallest man and then calculated the weight of water that must have fallen recently.

And now a few sums.

A cubic metre of water weighs a tonne.
A hectare is 100m x 100m.

So, one centimetre (which is $^1/_{100}$ of a metre) falling on a hectare will weigh: $100 \times 100 \times {}^1/_{100} = 100$ tonnes.

A centimetre of rain over a hectare weighs 100 tonnes.

A similar calculation for imperial measure arrives at 1 inch of rain over an acre is slightly greater than 100 tons (a ton and a tonne are about the same).

And now to the Yorkshire Wolds;

Over a square kilometre one centimetre of rain will weigh: $10 \times 10 \times 100 = 10,000$ tonnes. (10 hectares by 10 hectares by 100 tonnes).

The Wolds are about 1,300 Km^2 so each centimetre would deliver on to the Wolds: $1,300 \times 10,000$ tonnes $= 13m$ tonnes of water.

This year rainfall has been about 1.75 times the historic annual average, which is 21cm for the month.

In just this month, a staggering **275 million tonnes of rain** (275 million cubic metres); and all from fluffy clouds – isn't nature big?

Checking the figures using imperial measure.

2.54 cm = 1 inch.
21.0 cm = 8.25 inches.

Per acre this is about 825 tons.

640 acres to a square mile or 530,000m tons per square mile.

The Wolds at 1300 km^2 is c.500 square miles.

500 x 530,000m = 265m tons (pretty close to the metric figure).

We also learned that nature is big – and wet.

Thoughtfully, we headed home.

Walk 20. Bielby to Pocklington.

March 15th 2019 – remarkably windy (and has been for days).

A broken car, a broken taxi and a relatively short walk into Pocklington. The wind was relentless and we had chosen probably the only dry(ish) day of the fortnight, with regular storms off the Atlantic. We listened to the power lines and reminisced about why they hum. The daffs are now out and not to be confused with the waymarkers along the walk (thought we'd dropped that one).

With only one car we met at Selby station and drove a pretty but circuitous route into Pocklington for the start of the walk; we parked on York Road which was nearly our undoing on the return.

Bielby – the old water mill.

The start point was Bielby – a £10 cab ride and after ringing the four local taxi firms we found one that could pick us up – MNS Travel, a biggish car which was good and a reasonably cheerful driver. The other three taxi firms either failed to answer the phone, were broken down or didn't quite understand the concept of picking people up.

The start – canal left, drainage channel right.

We disembarked from the taxi with the old Church behind us –
saving that as the start point for another walk when we have two
cars; we set off between the overgrown canal and a full, and rushing,
drainage channel alongside the fields – lots of rain recently.

A bit like the fens.

The other side of the canal looked like the fens, pools of standing
water, flat land, wide vista.

After about a mile the path crosses the canal by one of those
clever Victorian Roving Bridges that are designed to let the boat-
horse cross from one bank to the other without having to disconnect
it from the barge.

Clever Victorian *Roving Bridge* – cross here.

From here to the head of the canal the main thing of note was the
wind and the effects of the wind; however, the hedgerow made a
remarkably efficient wind-break.

An efficient wind-break.
Note also the reeds – a constant feature.

As we passed under some power lines the wind was causing them to hum very noticeably, and as scientists (it says here) we spent probably twenty minutes advancing all manner of hypotheses (wound cable, harmonics, eddy currents, shape of insulators etc. etc.) but in the end were no wiser.

This academic noodling was brought to a sharp halt by a pigeon that flew about half way across the canal to be caught by a gust of wind and deposited unceremoniously back on the other bank – we'd never seen a bewildered pigeon before.

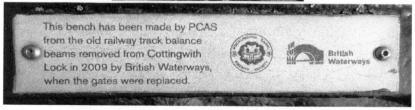

This bench has been made by PCAS from the old railway track balance beams removed from Cottingwith Lock in 2009 by British Waterways, when the gates were replaced.

British Waterways

Bench made out of bits of old railway.

After a couple of miles, passing a bench made from bits of railway, a number of locks in various states of repair spaced along a canal of varying degrees of dredging, we reached the canal head.

Is this where the ides for the stage show 'Warhorse' came from?

The canal head is easily recognised by the willow horse and a lot of signs saying "canal head".

The Wellington Oak on The York Road.

We are now on the York Road facing the Wellington Oak with no obvious path and nothing to indicate where Pocklington might be hiding.

There was then a debate about turning left or right along the York road to get to our parked car but, thankfully, sense prevailed and we had a look at the map (this is the bit mentioned earlier which was nearly our undoing).

On closer inspection of the grass verge over the road there is a 'path' to the right as you face the pub, past a farm gate to a second farm gate with a waymarker, which was not a daffodil, (the yard has shovels and forks nailed to the wall). Past a chap asleep in a grey van to try to get through the gate on the other side of the field and the path to Pocklington.

A grumpy looking horse was standing in what seemed to be the way so we went through the more obvious gate opposite to walk alongside the field, with All Saints Church in the distance providing a bit of reassurance.

We looked back at the gate we should have used – 6" of bog, broken, and secured with blue webbing. We had made the right choice.

'Gate', 6 inches of mud and a grumpy horse somewhere in the background.

The walk continues alongside fields to eventually emerge by a housing estate, with the path clearly marked between the houses.

Clearly marked path between houses.

To finally emerge into a well-tended graveyard which sat behind another graveyard.

A well-tended graveyard.

Through the graveyards, past two converted chapels to emerge around a couple of corners to face Aldi and Sainsbury.

Had we done the walk from the Pocklington end it is unlikely that we would have found the start.

And now for the cultural bit. Firstly, Pocklington itself – we have never seen a town with a scenic drive before.

And then on to All Saints Church, where people were clearing up after a school event, where we explored the stained glass and some seriously good woodcarving.

Outside the Church is the newly carved Sotheby Cross (the old part is inside the Church) put up to Sir John Sotheby whose descendants became the art auctioneers.

Woodcarving, sorry about the reflections.

The new bit and the old bit of the Sotheby Cross.

The Church has lots of fascinating history and artefacts; well worth the short time we spent there, but beer was now calling and back to the car – after discovering where Route 66 went (not sure if it's the one in the song though).

In the pub.

Sadly, only a shandy, bitter lemon and lemonade to get over the dehydration caused by the wind. Because we were driving and it was too early for dinner we took an early finish after planning the next bit, which seems to have quite a bit of upland and views over Millington village.

The wind had been relentless and was evidently the norm judging by the trees and reeds all at a funny angle. Thankfully, this wind was only in our faces part of the time, but we had learned to watch the weather forecast a bit more assiduously and plan the walks to have the wind at our backs. We also learned that pigeons can look bewildered.

Walk 21. Millington Wood to Pocklington.

Late October, after several weeks of excessive rain a beautiful start to the day. A taxi to Millington to walk backwards(!) to Pocklington; trees beginning to change colour, sunshine giving way to mist, a funny bench and an aerial view of feudalism.

Using public transport as much as possible we used one car to pick up at Selby where the incessant rain had turned fields into significant ponds on the way to Pocklington. Park. Bacon sandwiches and a call to the responsive taxi driver who had taken us to Bielby a few months earlier.

Past the nature reserve at Millington and a few hundred yards further on there is, on the right, the wooden bridge into the valley; walk to the wire fence and turn right up a steep hill opposite where we had emerged from the walk from the picnic area (Walk 22).

By now the bright sunshine which had been lifting the mist from the fields turned hazy, cool and clammy.

Sylvan Dale descending from the mist.

The uphill is, thankfully, soon over, ending in a gentle slope upwards past mushrooms and a few late flowers. In years gone by we would have managed this without breaking wind; today we're knackered.

**Mushrooms and
a lonely flower.**

The path follows the earthworks along the top of the valley to overlook Millington Bottom and the village of Millington; buzzards(?) circling overhead (and we're not dead yet).

Broad path overlooking Millington.

Lots of agriculture and rural pursuits with Warren Farm, its stables and land set aside to practise horse jumping, with some sad-looking horses (no doubt due to the weather).

Sad-looking horse – Eeyore please take note.

From up here Millington (through the mist) looks decidedly medieval, with a track leading down that is part of the Minster Way – not for us, we keep going along the top.

The village boasts a significant Church and a couple of big houses. Noticeable are what look like glebes – ancient parcels of land doled out by the Church to the villagers.

Millington Village, glebes in the foreground.

And now, our bit of culture for the day – a very strange bench – no doubt a significant work of art, and like all good art designed to make you think. Our only thoughts were "who created this rubbish?"

A daft bench and a smug Dave.

Two of the inscriptions read:

"Our breath it's song above springs as they pour a villa into village, marsh marigolds into God's chrysalis" what?

"The body's unfolding way from dale to dale. Our muscles burn in its common knowledge" Eh?

There's a couple more, but let's stop at these.

194

Soon after this artistic/poetic interlude, the path goes back on itself, Steve wanted to go straight on despite clear signage and a warning (he still can't find the butter in the fridge).

The sign clearly shouts 'Private Property'.

A sharp left and right, clearly marked on the map, alongside the woods above Warren Dale on a broad track which falls away to a minor road. The signpost by the roadside isn't too helpful; the wooden bits pointing to Nunburnholme which is miles out of the way.

The useful information is on the metal bits that you can't read from the descending path and which point the way for cyclists.

The helpful bit, on top – we're on the bench behind.

We're about half-way, so time for lunch and to try some American energy bars; seems 'crunchy' has now been redefined. Sycamore seeds are descending around us as we eat lunch and enjoy the view; no Steve, those sycamore are lime.

And onwards by road (Chalkland way and Wilberforce Way) to the hamlet of Kilnwick Percy where there's the Grade 2 listed hall which is now the Madhyamaka Buddhist Centre.

A little way along the road is the Kilnwick Percy hotel, golf course and other facilities (looks quite smart). This used to be part of the hall but now under separate ownership.

Signs to look out for.

The Chalkland Way, which we are now following, runs out of the familiar wooden sign posts and adopts the Pilgrimage of Grace Heritage Trail followed by big purple rectangles that guide across the less dangerous parts of the golf course.

The walk is pretty uneventful, wide and clearly marked (The Chalkland Way has a black swan as a marker), past a few more lonely flowers before descending into Pocklington shortly after a substantial display explaining the Pilgrimage of Grace which starts in Pocklington and zigzags through Kilnwick Percy and Nunburnholme before ending in Warter (names to conjure with).

Part of the display pointing out local features.

About here the Church of All Saints, which sits in the middle of Pocklington, becomes visible and provides that bit of confidence to choose a route back. The Church, also known as the Cathedral of the Wolds, is Grade 1 listed and dates back to the 12th century.

The way into Pocklington is quite convoluted and, like the Bielby section, would be tricky to navigate in the other direction.

We descended through a housing estate where a very helpful lady directed us right, left, left, right into a ginnel, across a small road, down, leftish, then right and after a bit fork left (the Church is now hidden behind houses and trees) and into Pocklington.

We thought a bit of time in the old Church again would be suitably cultural – but it was shut.

<u>In the pub.</u>

So back to the car and a short drive to Selby where we enjoyed Judson's pub, but as we were driving, we stuck to coffee from a cheerful barmaid, who really knew her job and wouldn't take any nonsense, followed by pie and chips. Excellent.

A day of some interest where we learned that a glebe is a medieval measure of land and that artistic benches can be quite unintelligible.

Walk 22. Picnic Area to Millington Wood.

September 2019 dry and windy.

A two-car exercise and a day of averages, cows block the way (several times), newly mowed fields, some quite steep bits, grouse beaters and an impressively well-tended nature reserve. A wide, clear path we travel in the reverse direction and, frankly, not too much to report other than peace and quiet.

The day started in Millington Nature Reserve where we had breakfast and then left one of the cars behind to drive to the start. Having missed the turning we pointed too far east and added a couple of extra miles turning back along the A166 to the picnic spot to begin the walk.

The start of this stretch is a quite boring mile or so of road; walking down the insignificant lane to the right that leads to Waterman Hole. The wind turbine is a good marker.

The wind turbine in the distance.

The walk starts by the woods just past the turbine.

Turn down the path opposite these odd gateposts.

Under (or round) the barrier.
(this picture is looking backwards).

And into the dark wood.

Out from the dark wood to follow a broad path with sheep on the hillside…

I know there are sheep somewhere over there.

… To be confronted by cows with calves, spread across the gate we needed to go through; so, a bit of gentle progress, no eye contact and (we hoped) the appearance of being in charge.

A broad path.

Safely through.

The helpful 'beware' sign is on the wrong side of the gate.

The path takes us over the lovely dry valleys that make up the Yorkshire Wolds; absolute peace (for the moment) and a gentle stroll where we could have been the only people on the planet.

Peace, space to think – brilliant.

Then more bloody cattle – a couple of truculent heifers. Same routine, appear confidently in charge, be gentle, no eye contact and through the gate; deep breath.

Try it on – if you think you're hard enough.

Following the valley, we come to the road that leads from Huggate to Millington through Pasture Dale. You can tell it's an important road by not much grass growing down the middle and the left-hand side slipping away only slightly (mind your sump).

The main road. (less grass down the middle).

Over the road and a few yards north there is a somewhat overgrown path to a gate and up a steep bit. It's quite hard to show in a photo how steep it is, but a couple of rests on the way up were welcome; then when we thought we'd made it, back down another steep hill and then up again.

Down and then back up.

And, all the time, more magnificent views over the Wolds; more peace, and more time for reflection (for the moment).

And up – the main road is down below.

And more cows – usual routine.

We're now at the highest point of this section of the walk, along a big field that has been harvested with the straw ready for baling and a hedgerow that keeps off quite a stiff wind. We thought about having lunch on a bench with a great view over the valley but reckoned the wind was probably strong enough to blow our meal away.

A well-tended broad path, hedgerow (wind break) to the right.

We passed quite a lot of wildlife ranging from a pair of kestrels in the distance, resting on an electric transmission line, peasants, phartidges and grice (one pretended to be poorly, so we walked past – usual routine, no eye contact, gentle movement, appear in charge).

And, as a poignant reminder about wildlife, down below was a person looking as if collecting insects with an orange thing on a stick and in the distance people were walking over the harvested field.

After a while it became evident that they were beaters whose job was to scare the living daylights out of the local wildlife and give the shoot, higher up the valley, something to aim at.

As we have lived mainly in towns and could not be considered posh in any way, this was quite a spectacle – people with bright orange things on sticks (orange so they didn't get shot?) and the bang-bang-bang of gunfire in the distance (peace now shattered, but on *average* a quiet day).

We only met two people on this walk, and very knowledgeable they were too; they introduced us to a number of plants and one of only two UK thistles with a scent (still no idea of its name). There were several blue flowers and a number of butterflies (no idea of their names either).

Wildlife.

And now, the descent. For the very brave – straight down. For us, a big zig-zag.

The path descends quite steeply into the valley.

Looking back, entering the zag. Great view.

Walking out of the valley we noticed that the bridge over the stream had had its planks replaced – someone actually cares and looks after things. This degree of consideration was very noticeable later in Millington Wood. Steps being recently replaced and path edges showing new wood; as did the view-point – must have been a bit of a trial getting all this stuff up so high.

Millington Wood.

An additional 1½ miles of culture. After a period of forestry operations, when ancient ash was replaced with Norway spruce, the local authority (which now owns the wood) is seeking to reverse this by replacing the conifers which are used to produce charcoal for sale locally.

Refreshment facilities consist of picnic tables in the car park, and the nearest public toilet is 4 miles away in Pocklington – we wondered how to cope with a five-year old bursting for a wee. The walk is mostly level – until the final ascent.

Gnarly tree near the start of the path.

We noted that the old ash trees have quite straight trunks – ideal for ships' masts. That ash, Steve, is Norway spruce.

The charcoal burner.

Path still quite level here – steps in the distance.

170 steps lead up to the view-point; these steps are set about one pace apart so by the time you get to the top, one leg is absolutely knackered, the other leg is OK though, so *on average*, they were fine.

Natural woods from just below the view-point.

Vista from the view-point (quite a climb).

Back to pick up the other car, turned a bit early, went too far west and added a few miles driving back east on the A166. But *on average* we got the road journey from Millington to the picnic area just right.

No pub this time but we did learn to respect cows and to appear brave – almost as if we knew what we were doing and learned that *average* is not always a good measure.

The weather was fine all day but quite variable, so here are some different types of cloud to finish this part of the walk.

Clouds.

Walk 23. Wharram Percy to the Picnic Area.

Or: 8 miles of peace and quiet.

And Several Churches.

In which public transport is quite sparse and we needed to take the two-car approach; really quiet and peaceful although a bit windy; took the better direction where the ups were short and steep, the downs were quite long and (from the other direction) relentless. Met a truly miserable landlady, couldn't find the hidden art but did find the landscape sculpture. Culture was two of Sir Tatton Sykes' Churches at the end of the walk and a really good pub meal to finish.

The day started with the (now customary) bacon sandwich in the picnic area about three miles east of Fridaythorpe on the A166 (GR 834572, OS Explorer 294).

We left Steve's car there and Dave drove us to the car park above Wharram Percy where we start the day. Last time we were here we headed north; today we head south to Thixendale and beyond.

A beautiful day for a walk.

We walk down the track where we saw the filming described later in Walk 24 (because we didn't do things in sequence), into and through Wharram Percy to the old pond, along the left-hand bank to a sign pointing to the Centenary Way.

Through a kissing gate with an unnecessary ***Please shut the gate*** sign attached, to walk up to the ridge where we could see the trees that would mark the junction where we joined the Yorkshire Wolds Way.

From the ridge we saw what looked like a road in the valley; this looked like quite large, irregular pieces of limestone for a tractor or to herd cattle; whatever their purpose they are painful to walk over, so we made the decision to head upwards and follow the crest of the valley.

Looking down Deepdale valley.
The marker trees are on the horizon.

We are now in the Wolds proper; not a person to be seen, no aeroplanes, no traffic and, now that the harvest is in, nothing in the way of agricultural vehicles or shooting parties. Peace.

Peace – and winter wheat?

On the ridge we could not help but notice the wind right now, which the weather forecast told us was due to arrive later in the day.

Steve has a touch of the wind.

Then through a field of heifers that looked quite threatening but as there was no alternative path, we adopted the managerial "I'm in charge around here" posture, whilst recognising that this was their field and that each of them weighed about half a ton. After a certain amount of mutual respect, we passed by uneventfully.

Heifer standing ground – the others don't seem too bothered.

From the various books and write-ups it appears we are about to enter a rather artistic bit of England – David Hockney worked here extensively, Robert Fuller's gallery is nearby, there are about twelve pieces of hidden art and also landscape art – plenty for everybody.

The aim of art has been noted as to stimulate us and cause us to see things in a different light but sometimes this can be difficult to appreciate; not many would walk the 45 miles to Hessle as shown on the imaginative milepost.

**Is this art, a half-way marker, a joke, or an excuse
to put up something a bit phallic for the kids to snigger at?**

The path goes for about a mile of trees when there is a path to the left which leads into the eastern end of Thixendale and is signed Centenary Way and Chalkland Way.

We ignored this and continued for about another mile to a path on the left signed Wolds Way and Centenary Way which takes us into the eastern end of Thixendale.

Nice and level along a field edge, well marked path to a metal gate and what looked like the original gate to the path down the valley; but overgrown and impossible to access. Through the gate to the right and stay high along the top of the valley.

Looks as if the way was originally to the left (it was).

In reality, the path is in the bottom of the valley, as we discovered, looking backwards after seeing the first of only five hikers during the entire walk.

Nevertheless, we continued along the high ground and later descended easily at the foot of the valley – this was our obligatory 'take a wrong turning' moment. The bottom of this valley is also the bottom of Vessey Hill which is quite steep and where we met four kindred spirits walking down towards us.

Looking back from Vessey Hill.
The path is in the valley – not up in those trees!

After a bit of puffing and panting we reached the summit – quite short but also quite steep when the path levels out along a field edge before turning gently right to lead us into Thixendale.

Apparently, there are earthworks and tumuli around this point but we missed them; possibly hidden in the woods that line the broad track.

Allegedly there is a *Secret Art Point* just past Cow Wold Barn as the broad track begins its descent into the village. We missed that too – evidently kept suitably secret.

Confusingly, there are two Thixen Dales; this one leads into the top of the village; and after walking through the village we enter the other Thixen Dale to continue the journey.

'Upper' Thixen Dale.

The village appears laid out before us, the manor house immediately below and most of the houses and buildings positioned along the single road. Our way through the village lay straight ahead.

Thixendale appears from around a corner.

This is the central part of the walk; Thixendale is at the convergence of six (big) dales and sixteen (little) dales – remote, quiet and left alone.

The Church was built in the late 1800s and is one that Sir Tatton Sykes restored along with Fridaythorpe and Garton-on-the-Wolds which we visit later.

The school subsequently became a youth hostel and is now the village hall. Mains water didn't arrive until 1930 and the original hand pump is at the top of the village. Wonder if it still works?

Youth Hostel, school, village hall.

It's now getting towards lunch time and the bacon sandwiches have worn off, so the idea of a sit-down in the local pub seemed a good idea. It's on the left as you leave the village and set back quite a bit; so, approaching the lady working in the garden to politely enquire if the hostelry was serving.

We met with a resounding 'No!' – perhaps she was having an off day. Reminded us of *George and the Dragon* by Stanley Holloway, so fearsome that we didn't have the courage to ask if George was in or if we could sit at one of her under-employed picnic tables.

Out of the village, turn right; a road goes back on us to Fridaythorpe, shortly after there is a fork where we kept to the right (signed Robert Fuller Gallery) and into 'Lower Thixen Dale'.

A signpost directs us across fields and into the valley where we start to prospect for somewhere to enjoy lunch; there are earthworks around here but we missed them too.

Eventually found a log; which was elm and by now as hard as rock; should be there for millennia. While we ate lunch, we noticed the trees showed an interesting phenomenon normally seen in planted fields where growth is in waves; taller plants keeping light from those next to them, and as they get shorter more light gets through and so the next ones can grow tall – and so it continues.

Waves of trees in 'Lower' Thixen Dale; nice clouds.

The gate at the bottom led into a broader valley where there must be some interesting nature as indicated by a big hide up a tree, various nesting boxes and smaller hides tucked away on the hillside (Robert Fuller?)

It's in this valley that the Yorkshire Wolds Way doubles back on itself and where we keep straight on along the public footpath which hasn't yet been given a name as far as we could tell.

Follow 'Public Footpath'.
(image has been brightened up a bit).

The public footpath leads to the one bit of art we did manage to find that day; landscape art that looks like a maze (but isn't) with a path in and a path out, another example is a few yards away up the hill.

216

Landscape Art – it's quite big.
That's David stood on the second ring.

Out of 'Lower' Thixen Dale and into Bradeham Dale. The path continues past Bradeham Well and into the dark woods which are Wayrham Dale and the last part of today's walk.

Bradeham Dale sports the only standing water we saw all day, marked on the map as Bradeham Well. We surmised that the well was named after a person called Bradeham who probably didn't live very long, judging by the scum and crap floating in the thing.

Bradeham Well.

Then into the woods that mark Wayrham Dale and which appeared very dark after a day of walking into the sunshine.

We came out of the trees for a short way where the path diverged: to the right into Fordham Dale, left into in Wayrham Dale; we kept left and back into the gloom.

And into the dark wood.

Along the way, driving here and also at home we have noted that a number of plants think it's spring: irises out in Thixendale, crocuses in Malton and now a dandelion that has gone all the way to seed – funny old biological world isn't it?

A dandelion clock.

Emerging into full sunlight we could hear traffic and realised we were near journey's end. A broad track leads to the A166; a bit of care crossing and back to the car park with enough time for some proper culture.

218

Back in the dim and distant a gentleman called Sir Tatton Sykes (whose descendants still live in Sledmere House) decided that a number of local Churches could do with a bit of TLC so he built, rebuilt or restored no fewer than eighteen of them.

One is St. Mary in Thixendale which we passed earlier; it was built in the 1870s and which saved the walk over the hills to Wharram Percy (which must have been a bit of a bind in winter).

Two others are St Mary in Fridaythorpe and St. Michael & All Angels in Garton-on-the-Wolds. We decided to visit these latter two as our cultural interlude.

St. Mary, Fridaythorpe is about 1,000 years old with contemporary features including the archway over the door with the dogtooth carving. There was damage over the ages and significant restoration and renovation in 1902-3 when the distinctive clock was added to the Norman tower.

St. Mary - the main doorway.

Inside the Church there are a number of antiquities: an old bell from around the 16th century and the font is from around 1100AD.

C.16 Bell.   **C.11 Font.**

There is some excellent stained glass and carvings; the carved alter screen came from Sledmere Church in 1895 during restoration.

The carved alter screen.

The clockwork can be seen behind the font and was installed in the early 1900s; this drives the distinctive clock.

The clockwork.

The distinctive clock with the inscription:
"Time is short: Eternity is Long"

Another cheery Victorian inscription.

Now to Garton-on-the-Wolds.

St. Michael and All Angels in Garton has probably the most amazing collection of wall and ceiling paintings in a UK parish Church; they were completed in 1876. Over time water, dust and the smoke from the coke heater rendered them black and unrecognisable (according to the knowledgeable gentleman who we bumped into).

The Nikolaus Pevsner Trust agreed to undertake the restoration of the paintings in Sir Nikolaus' memory.

Recognition of Sir Nikolaus.

There has also been significant (and very highly professional) restoration to the outside of the Church.

The dog-tooth entrance.

The nave – the photograph doesn't do justice to the painting.

The ceiling – painted like a fairground (very Victorian).

A row of ugly little beggars outside.

And no prettier in close-up.

<u>Medieval time-keeping – thumbdials,</u>

Used by the vicar to time the start of the (interminable?) service. Could it be that in medieval times people prayed for rain, or at least for a cloudy day?

Garton has quite well defined hours.

Fridaythorpe not so well defined.

In the pub.

Soft drinks again because we were driving. The pub served an excellent meal which we thoroughly enjoyed with quite a lot to look back on: landscape art and how big it is, and the amazing jobs done restoring local Churches and learned about thumbdials which presumably pre-date clocks.

Planning the next bit, we decided to make it a shortish walk in order to be able to spend some time in Wharram Quarry Nature Reserve which is on the route and famous for butterflies and some quite rare plants.

Walk 24. Wharram Percy to N. Grimston.

And Wharram Quarry Nature Reserve.

A day in which we took in the deserted village; some years ago, Dave (who could drive a plane) had flown over it and wanted to see it at ground level; chatted to a film crew and visited one of the best nature reserves in the area.

On leaving the car park we descended the steep 1st century path to Wharram Percy, which nestles in a picturesque valley, the first sight is a brick-built structure which is used by the archaeologists and others who are still exploring the site (one of the most studied sites in England), and behind the brick building, the eye goes directly to the remains of St. Martin's Church.

St. Martin's ruined Church.

In past times the village had been a farming community with two mills. After a series of 'adventures' (well worth reading up on the English Heritage website) the earnings from the water-driven corn mills and fish from the millponds were replaced by the landowner by more profitable grazing sheep. The fields were turned from arable to grazing and the population dwindled.

Millpond with St. Martin's behind.

There are numerous 'footprints' of deserted dwellings but unfortunately they don't lend themselves to very good photographs.

So, having had our fill of archaeology it was time to head north along the old L & NE railway that connected Malton and Driffield. It had been managed by Charles Dickens' brother (who lived in Norton) and then closed by Richard Beeching in the 1960s, thereby cutting off Burdale, Fimber and Wetwang from civilisation.

The old railway tunnel emerged at Wharram Percy and the overgrown banking was being used by a film crew, apparently because it's a bit like Normandy.

Lots of standing around.
– and a couple of people off-picture being a bit precious.

A nice clear track which goes past the quarry where the stone was taken to create the railway embankments – we couldn't find the southern entrance.

Wharram Quarry Nature Reserve.

Past the decaying platforms that must have been an old stop and out onto the road leading quite steeply uphill to Wharram Street.

Climbing the hill, on the right-hand side is the northern entrance to Wharram Quarry Nature Reserve through the five-barred gate.

This nature reserve is home to all manner of butterflies and wild flowers; some quite rare, and one or two parasitic plants.

Butterflies & Flowers – the photos don't do the place justice.

We met a lovely couple out for the day with fold-up chairs, a flask of coffee and a picnic who pointed out some of the more interesting features – seems that they came here quite a lot for the peace and quiet.

228

After sticking to the paths in the nature reserve and taking lots of photos we bade farewell to the picnicking couple, back through the main gate and back to the disused railway.

A disused railway and a disused house.

A couple of gentle miles later we arrived in North Grimston to emerge along the path into the village centre that would be the start of the final leg into Malton.

Fancied a pint – the pub (Middleton Arms) was shut.

We hadn't allowed for rubbish telephone reception here, so to call a taxi involved standing on things and leaning round corners in the vain hope of communicating. Thankfully, we eventually succeeded.

In the pub.

Back into Norton, then over the river to Malton for a gentle pint and a light meal where David was told in no uncertain terms that he was unbelievably ugly – by a middle-aged lady who had made herself quite vivacious and attractive (to herself no doubt) through the application of significant quantities of alcohol.

The next bit is the conclusion of the walk and into Malton again – hopefully avoiding the spirited lady.

Walk 25. North Grimston to Malton.

We complete the journey from Derby; this bit was planned as a leisurely start, pub lunch and an easy walk. where we reflect, marvel at meanders, follow a closed railway line, pass horse racing stables, rest by a duck pond and finish the saga with some excellent beer.

We're in North Yorkshire this morning, on the last leg of the journey to Malton from North Grimston (only in Yorkshire do you get such evocative place names). This is a shortish walk when we had the idea to start with a pub lunch. Paul the taxi driver picked us up in Malton and dropped us at the local hostelry.

The Middleton Arms for lunch.
It was shut!

Not to worry, we're professionals and familiar with venues out in the country where places close for lunch. We made an executive decision to take a longer walk and save the refreshments for later.

This walk was a bit different from our earlier walks: firstly, we arrived at the start by taxi. Steve, of course, though a Yorkshireman, has lived in the Thames Valley, so is into this sort of stuff.

David, on the other hand, is blessed with a free rail pass so hasn't seen the inside of a taxi for most of his life. Dave has worked all over the place, mostly in obscure places that can only be reached by car, motorbike, bicycle or horse.

Being true Yorkshiremen rather than part-infused southerners (like Steve) taxis are regarded as an unnecessary expense and ever so slightly indulgent, if not downright expensive and decadent.

Following the road back to Malton for a couple of hundred yards the start of the Centenary Way is clearly marked by the side of a broad track that heads off to the right.

An aside: some of this walk appears to be over farmland, by concession of the landowner, so time of year can be important because the path can be obscured by cows & a bull, sheep & lambs, horses and very protective (read "professionally aggressive") dogs.

The land is flat around here, and if you look at the stream on the map it meanders somewhat, that's sort of in keeping with the spirit of these walks.

The meandering Settrington Beck.

The path follows the beck almost as far as Settrington; a little way into the walk we narrowly avoided being mown down by a high-speed tractor towing a muck cart, our guess was that the velocity leaves the odour behind. It certainly seemed to work.

The beck pays tribute to the accuracy of the OS map which shows it's meanders quite clearly. The scenery is open and pleasant, the path can be a bit indistinct at times but gates, stiles and waymarkers kept us on track for the mile or so to where we join a wide track. The point to turn up to the track is where a number of footbridges cross the beck.

One of the footbridges across the beck.

The way here is made quite clear by the number of 'prohibited' 'Keep Out' and 'Private' signs to keep us on track; past the house and along an easy and pleasant trail to a metalled road. Turn right along the road towards Settrington to be faced by the local school which is on the T-junction where we turned left past the Town Green.

The local school.

We followed the road past a row of distinctive houses to where the road turns left and the Centenary Way goes straight on.

Distinctive houses.
The route continues straight on in the distance.

The path is very well marked by a big and obvious signpost, and is wide and easy to follow along the edges of fields; after a short way there's a bear right, but this is up to a farm; keep straight on to where there is a signpost indicating a path that runs through woodlands and parallel to the main walk.

Both tracks meet up again at the edge of a field with a clear path to what used to be a railway line explained by Wikipedia that it was *"... served by Settrington railway station on the Malton and Driffield Railway between 1853 and 1950."* We couldn't blame Dr. Beeching for the closure because he wasn't doing his stuff until 15 years later. We worked out that this was a bit more of the railway line that used to be maintained by Charles Dickens' brother Alfred.

Tucked away on the left is a wooden bridge over a stream that leads onto the disused railway line.

The wooden bridge to the disused railway.

Are you sure it's the right way up?

A very easy short walk comes out at a sort of crossroads for tracks. Turning left we passed the waymarker for the Centenary Way which goes directly to Norton, and ignored it.

Turning left along this broad track.

Rather than go through Norton we decided there is a longer and more interesting way into Malton (our final destination) so we now left the Centenary Way behind and continued to the farm up ahead.

We know we're coming into racing country because the fields are full of horses instead of the usual sheep and cows that had blessed the earlier parts of the walk.

Horses.

Past the horses – which ignored us, and into the farmyard where we were assailed by a very noisy dog which chose not to ignore us, and: no, we're not playing with you.

A noisy dog; quieter one in the background.

Carrying on through the farmyard and up to the road; a right turn up the gently sloping hill with views over the countryside (the road was busier than we had expected, being in the middle of nowhere) to come to a T-junction on the Beverley Road.

Over the road and on to the bridleway which runs parallel to the road for a very short distance before veering left. Great views over the fields, St. Peter's Church in the middle distance.

Easy walking for about a mile.

Past more horses and stables – some very successful.

View over the gallops.

Done very well.

Eventually the bridleway decants us onto Langton Road, turn right for a short distance to then turn left down Bazleys Lane (or even Bazeley's Lane, depending on the map), past more stables, when the left-hand side of the road opens out with quite a steep slope upwards.

Steepish slope up to the conservation area.

Up the slope and turn right into woods; there is a parallel path that goes along field edges but the woods are more atmospheric and interesting when, about half a mile further, the path slopes gently downwards to re-join Bazleys Lane just before the Whitewall Stables.

Where's Thelwell?

236

Out on to the main road before the last mile or so to complete the journey. There's a helpful signpost telling us that Pocklington is only 31 miles from Malton.

Pretty sure we walked more than 30 miles to get here!

After a bit of a discussion whether the signpost is correct, the end is in sight with a walk down a pleasant road, houses to one side, fields to the other.

About half way down the hill there's a wedding business (shown on Google maps as Brooklands Vintage Cars where a couple of old classics (no, not us) were parked outside, we walked slowly past them reminiscing about our childhoods when cars had a bit of shape.

A couple of old classics, we walked slowly by.

A brief detour to the duck pond (or Lakeside Gardens to you and me) to gather our strength for the final descent into Malton and the finale to our adventure.

The Duck Pond.

Back onto the road, downhill, past Lidl and the used car garage, over the level crossing to look down at the other River Derwent, turn left and follow the river downstream along the Riverside Walk through the picnic garden that has been known to flood. In the rainy season, the Derwent here can rise from a depth of about two feet to over twelve feet. The record depth was 16 feet 6 inches (5.03m) in 2000.

Norton's Riverside Walk.

Emerging at the picnic garden's far end, we turned right over the bridge up the slope into Malton and, feeling smug, journey's end.

<u>In the pub.</u>

The Brass Castle – Journey's End.
Brewery, taphouse, good company.

A lot of self-congratulation, perhaps too much good beer, no-one telling us we were ugly, and the opportunity to look back on a walk a month that lasted for more than two years – each walk being a bit of organising for one of us and a day's holiday for the other two. Very worthwhile.

Another toast to Wainwright, a resolution to do something similar again and to publish what has been a very companiable and enjoyable journey in the hope that anyone reading about our walk will enjoy good company and this (or a similar) journey as much as we have.

In Conclusion.

So, we created what began as a possibility over a pint, explored a number of options and decided to follow the advice of Wainwright in his book *A Coast to Coast Walk* and to make up the journey as we went.

Fortunately, we had ready-made points joining our homes which are strung out across the North of England so we could manage much with public transport, minimise driving and maximise the social aspects of our getting together again after many years.

Perhaps fitting to close with the words of Alfred Wainwright in his concluding personal notes:

"... Insofar as they [official long-distance footpaths] get people into the fresh air, well and good, for urban existence today demands an occasional change of environment; insofar as they provide a challenge, well and good, for a life without challenges is tedious. But the wide publicity given to them brings disadvantages. The official blessing and openness of a long-distance path is headline news. The word goes forth and the world pulls on his boots.

The first of them, the Pennine Way has already been so much used that it is fast losing its original appeal as a wilderness walk and becoming a too-popular parade. There are blazed tracks and litter where there once there were neither. Some paths are so badly eroded that diversions have been necessary ... In time you won't need a map: just follow the trail of empty cans and orange peel.

... The trouble is that officially prescribed routes cannot be selective of their users. They are open to all. They invite all. They are used by all.

You don't need to have an official route to get you out into the open air. You don't have to wait for the Countryside Commission to say 'O.K. you can go. You don't have to follow the crowds. In this country there are thousands of long-distance routes for walkers that have never suffered an official blessing (and are all the better for that) and any walkers with initiative can plan his own itineraries simply by linking the public rights of way recorded on current issues of the ... Ordnance maps.

Alfred Wainwright 1973.

Personal Log.

In the cities the grid reference is normally the railway station where we met to begin that part of the walk.

Section 1: Derby to Chesterfield.

Diversion	Start/Finish	Map	Grid ref.	Date
	Derby	OS 259	362 255	
	Belper	OS 259	348 476	
Crich Trams		OL 24	246 549	
Holloway		OL 24	327 562	
	Whatstandwell	OL 24	333 541	
Duffield (EVR)		OS 259	246 436	
Wirksworth		OL 24	290 540	
Stone Centre		OL 24	288 552	
	Cromford	OL 24	299 571	
Hts. of Abraham		OL 24	292 586	
	Matlock	OL 24	297 602	
St. Helen's Ch.		OL 24	661 255	
	Baslow	OL 24	256 724	
	Wadshelf	OL 24	318 709	
	Chesterfield	OS 269	388 714	

241

Diversion		Start/Finish	Map	Grid ref.	Date
		Chesterfield	OS 269	388 714	
Barrow Hill			OS 269	413 755	
Beer Festival	▼				
		Halfway	OS 278	350 881	
	▼				
		Sheffield Centre	OS 278	358 872	
Kelham Island			OS 278	350 881	
	▼				
		Meadowhall	OS 278	390 192	
Wentworth					
Woodhouse	▼		OS 278	396 977	
	▲	Elsecar	OS 278	387 999	
		Conisborough	OS 279	509 995	
	▼	Doncaster	OS 279	571 035	
	▲				
		Braithwaite	OS 279	621 127	
	▼	Snaith	OS 290	642 222	
	▼	**Selby**	OS 290	618 322	

Diversion		Start/Finish	Map	Grid ref.	Date
	▲	**Selby**	OS 290	618 322	
Selby Abbey			OS 290	616 324	
	▲	Wressle	OS 291	710 312	
	▲	Holme-on-Spalding-Moor	OS 291	798 390	
Market Weighton			OS 294	879 417	
		Bielby	OS 294	789 437	
	▼				
	▲	Pocklington	OS 294	802 490	
Millington Reserve			OS 294	839 531	
	▲	A166 Picnic area	OS 294	835 568	
		Wharram Percy	OS 300	859 643	
Churches					
	▼	North Grimston	OS 300	843 678	
Wharram Quarry			OS 300	858 653	
	▼	**Malton**	OS 300	785 715	

243

Walk 4½. Matlock & Cromford Mill.

This part of the walk is only about a mile and a half. It had been set aside as a day of culture and coincidentally would have landed in April around Dave and Steve's birthdays, the idea was a leisurely visit to a number of attractions and end the day sipping beer by the river with a nice meal to round things off whilst planning the next adventure.

Sadly, not to be. The coronavirus Covid-19 has prompted the government to close pubs, bars and restaurants; dissuade us all from public transport, recommend we stay at home, and only go out if really essential – even fresh air isn't safe.

This unfinished part of the walk will take place when we have: herd immunity, vaccines and permission to travel.

There is an impressive list of cultural places to pick from – depending on weather and terrain; these include:

The Peak District Mining Museum.

Gulliver's Kingdom.

Derwent Gardens.

Cable car to the Heights of Jacob.

Matlock Bath.

The aquarium.

Wildcat Crag.

Harp Edge woods.

Various nature reserves.

And, of course, Arkwright's Mill.

An awful lot of culture in a mile and a half.

Index of places and pubs

The End

Wherever next?

Ingram Content Group UK Ltd.
Milton Keynes UK
UKHW020435310323
419426UK00004B/10